Research-practice Partnerships for School Improvement

Research-practice Partnerships for School Improvement: The Learning Schools Model

BY

MEI KUIN LAI
The University of Auckland, New Zealand

STUART McNAUGHTON
The University of Auckland, New Zealand

REBECCA JESSON
The University of Auckland, New Zealand

AARON WILSON
The University of Auckland, New Zealand

United Kingdom – North America – Japan – India – Malaysia – China

Emerald Publishing Limited
Howard House, Wagon Lane, Bingley BD16 1WA, UK

First edition 2020

Reprints and permissions service
Contact: permissions@emeraldinsight.com

British Library Cataloguing in Publication Data
A catalogue record for this book is available from the British Library

ISBN: 978-1-78973-572-7 (Print)
ISBN: 978-1-78973-571-0 (Online)
ISBN: 978-1-78973-573-4 (Epub)

Printed and bound by CPI Group (UK) Ltd, Croydon, CR0 4YY

ISOQAR certified
Management System,
awarded to Emerald
for adherence to
Environmental
standard
ISO 14001:2004.

Certificate Number 1985
ISO 14001

INVESTOR IN PEOPLE

Contents

List of Figures and Tables

Figures

Tables

About the Authors

Mei Kuin Lai (PhD) is an Associate Professor at the Faculty of Education and Social Work, and an Associate Director at the Woolf Fisher Research Centre, The University of Auckland. Her research focusses on research-practice partnerships to improve valued student outcomes, in particular, how collaborative analysis of data in professional learning communities and networks contribute to these improvements. She was the joint-recipient of the University of Auckland's Research Excellence Award (2015), awarded for research of demonstrable quality and impact, for her work in co-designing and co-testing the Learning Schools Model. She has published in journals like *Teaching and Teacher Education* and *Reading Research Quarterly,* where her first authored article was selected for inclusion in the International Literacy Association's edited book, *Theoretical models and processes of reading (6th Edition).* She consults nationally and internationally, and has led or co-led large-scale and regional projects in New Zealand.

Stuart McNaughton (ONZM, PhD) is a Professor of Education at the Faculty of Education and Social Work and the former Director of the Woolf Fisher Research Centre, The University of Auckland. He is also New Zealand's Chief Education Scientific Advisor. He has published extensively on children's literacy and language development, the design of effective educational programmes for culturally and linguistically diverse populations and cultural processes in development. He is a recipient of research prizes, consults on curricula and educational interventions nationally and internationally and has a position as Distinguished Overseas Professor at East China Normal University (Shanghai). He is a member of the International Reading Hall of Fame for sustained contributions to literacy research, literacy leadership and the preparation of leaders in the literacy field through teaching. He was the joint-recipient of the University of Auckland's Research Excellence Award (2015) for his work in co-designing and co-testing the Learning Schools Model. His publications have featured in journals such as *Reading Research Quarterly*.

Rebecca Jesson (PhD) is an Associate Professor at the Faculty of Education and Social Work, and an Associate Director at the Woolf Fisher Research Centre, The University of Auckland. Rebecca's research interests centre on literacy learning, and on developing effective instruction for all students that leads to advanced literacy skills. Most recently this focus has extended to investigating teaching and learning processes in Pacific Nations and within digital interventions in

New Zealand. Rebecca has led or co-led large Learning Schools Model projects reaching over 200 schools across three Pacific nations and in New Zealand. She was the joint-recipient of the University of Auckland's Research Excellence Award (2015) for her work in co-designing and co-testing the Learning Schools Model. She has published in journals like *Teaching and Teacher Education.*

Aaron Wilson (PhD) is the Associate Dean (Research) at the Faculty of Education and Social Work, and an Associate Director of the Woolf Fisher Research Centre, The University of Auckland. He researches and writes mainly about literacy, particularly disciplinary and adolescent literacy, as well as about teacher professional learning and development. He was the joint-recipient of the University of Auckland's Research Excellence Award (2015) for his work in co-designing and co-testing the Learning Schools Model. He presents and consults both locally and internationally, working with practitioners, policy-makers and researchers including the NZ Ministry of Education, and has led or co-led high profile large-scale projects. He was a Department Head for the Literacy Leadership Department of the *Journal of Adolescent and Adult Literacy*. He has published in journals such as *Reading Research Quarterly*.

The authors wish to acknowledge the Māori name for the Woolf Fisher Research Centre, Te Pūtahi Whakatairanga Hapori Ako Angitu (The Centre for the Promotion of Successful Learning Communities).

Foreword

Research-practice partnerships (RPPs) constitute a novel and valuable model for doing educational research, one that is growing in importance and in vitality. I celebrate that shift and greatly value the information presented in this book about one successful instantiation of the RPP model. We have come a long way beyond the metaphors 'applied research' and 'translation from research to practice' that dominated educational researchers' thinking as recently as 20 years ago.

I have myself worked in those more traditional models, developing tools that proved their worth in experimental trials but then were handed off to teachers who never used them. The difference in uptake when we can provide tools to solve problems that teachers themselves nominate is enormous and deeply gratifying. Thus, I am a strong supporter. The partnership approach of developing tools in response to practitioner needs (and to the extent possible in collaboration with practitioners) is much more effective in leading to high-quality implementation, to measurable impacts and to sustainability.

The intuitive appeal of this common sense approach should not, though, blind us to the risks associated with it. The sudden popularity of the RPP model, and the consequent expansion of funding for research carried out in this tradition, threatens to transform a very good idea into a fashion or a trend. Thus the RPP label is now used for many different approaches to doing educational work in the real world, not all of which are equally authentic exemplars. We should be cautious not to let the heterogeneity of what people are calling RPPs dilute the construct and obscure the importance of the central principles, which are so well incorporated into the work presented in this volume, on the Learning Schools Model (LSM).

This model displays particularly robustly one of the basic RPP principles – that the work be done locally, with a rich understanding of the context. In the work of the Strategic Education Research Partnership (SERP; www.serp.org), with which I have been involved, we have found that approaches to an urgent problem of practice developed for a specific school district always end up being useful to and adopted by other districts, sometimes but not always with minor tweaks. In other words, as discussed extensively in Chapter Seven of this book, working locally does not mean jettisoning the potential for broader impact, or for contributing to research knowledge. But anticipating those more global contributions prematurely can undermine the local commitment.

In the SERP work we have experienced many of the tensions and challenges associated with adopting the RPP approach, some of which are brilliantly illustrated for the New Zealand context in this volume:

- SERP is committed to starting with the practitioners' definition of the problem, but sometimes find that characterisation is not helpful. For example, in our early work in the Boston Public Schools we were asked by the superintendent to 'solve' the problem of middle-grades reading comprehension. The teachers, on the other hand, characterised the challenge as academic vocabulary – a much more tractable issue. We found, after many years of work, that tools to improve academic vocabulary did indeed improve reading comprehension (Jones et al., 2019), but had we started focussing on interventions for reading comprehension itself we might never have gotten there.
- The collaborative data analysis that is a core practice in the LSM is costly in time and can limit the sophistication of the analyses. An alternative model, adopted within the longstanding partnership between the Department of Early Childhood at the Boston Public Schools (DECBPS) and a team at the University of Michigan headed by Christina Weiland (Weiland, Sachs, McCormick, Hsueh, & Snow, in press) displays an alternative, in which Weiland's advanced quantitative analytic capacities are deployed to answer urgent DECBPS questions, such as whether investment in summer school for lagging students was justified. Collaboration focussed on refining the question to that BPS got the answer it needed, rather than on engaged in the actual analytic process.
- The LSM centres its activities inside schools, with a focus on professional learning and development as the lever for improvement. SERP also works inside schools, but has focussed its efforts on developing tools that are immediately useful to teachers and that have the potential to change classroom practice; many of the SERP tools are designed to 'carry the training with them,' in part because the organisation does not have the capacity to deliver professional development at large scale. Other robust RPPs have focussed much more outside schools on structural and policy issues. The Chicago Consortium for School Research, for example, and the New York City Research Alliance have access to district data and respond to district requests for specific analyses, but also develop their own questions in discussion with the district. Collaboration in these cases is characterised by regular communication and adherence to a 'no surprises' rule before findings are made public. But the basic model of educational improvement puts more emphasis on district and school policies than the RPPs that do their work mostly with teachers, inside schools. A recurrent challenge, and one that the LSM team has solved brilliantly, is the sustainability of the partnership model. In the US context, where individual districts have considerable autonomy, where the tenure of district leaders rarely lasts more than a few years, and where new leadership is free to bring in new practices and curricula, the work that is needed to keep partnerships alive across transitions is daunting, and not always successful. There are great advantages to systems of education more like New Zealand's, where there are fewer layers

between schools and central government and centralisation of curriculum and policies, which can promote a level of coherence that is rarely reached in US public schooling.

In short, this book can be read in many ways: as a primer in the advantages of RPPs as a new structure for engaging in educational research; as an analysis of the epistemological underpinnings of reliable knowledge about educational practice; as an encouraging story about educational improvement; and as a demonstration that lasting improvement in any complex system requires an unending cycle of learning how to learn.

by
Catherine Snow, PhD
Patricia Albjerg Graham Professor, Harvard Graduate School of Education
President of the American Educational Research Association (1999–2000)
Chair, Committee on the Prevention of Reading Difficulties in Young Children,
National Research Council, National Academy of Sciences, USA (1995–1998)

Acknowledgments

Nāu te rourou, nāku te rourou, ka ora ai te iwi
(With your basket and my basket, the people will thrive)
Māori Proverb

To our school, policy, research, and community partners,
and to those who support them

To our families

Chapter One

Ambitious Aims: Research for Solutions and Knowledge

Improving educational practice while advancing research knowledge is a lofty aim. Meeting these twin objectives is fundamentally important yet difficult to achieve in practice, particularly when the focus is on meaningful and lasting changes in educational outcomes in schools. The literature is awash with cautionary tales of research having little impact on practice. Yet there are pressing problems in school effectiveness and in particular, inequities between groups of students, that feel intractable. Both between and within countries we can see ongoing patterns of disparities at the same time as we can see shining examples of effective practices (OECD, 2015).

Educational research should be contributing better to solutions. The reasons why it has not are, in part, due to the questionable relevance of educational research to practice (Snow, 2015, 2016). They also reflect just how difficult educational challenges are; five of which are variability, scalability, capability, acceleration and sustainability. These pose substantial challenges for researchers in school reform; and much has been written about them.

It is in this landscape that our work germinated. Our motivation as researchers is twofold: to improve the valued outcomes for students, primarily from culturally and linguistically diverse communities, who have been historically under-served in education; and to advance research knowledge both locally and internationally. We have not been able to do this without a real partnership with the local communities, schools and students, respecting and drawing on their expertise in the design and implementation of the joint work. These motivations have culminated in a whole-school intervention model called the 'Learning Schools Model' (LSM), a design-based research-practice partnership that has been tested and replicated over 15 years and across diverse contexts and countries. This book provides a research- and theory-informed, yet practical account of the model and its application across contexts.

In this introductory chapter, we begin by positioning our work within the global challenges facing whole school interventions and within the wider call for different approaches to partnering with schools to improve practice and

Research-practice Partnerships for School Improvement:
The Learning Schools Model, 1–15
Copyright © 2020 by Mei Kuin Lai, Stuart McNaughton, Rebecca Jesson and Aaron Wilson
Published under exclusive license
doi:10.1108/978-1-78973-571-020201002

outcomes. We provide compelling reasons for adopting these new approaches, before describing how our book contributes to addressing the current gaps and avenues for future research in the current literature on these approaches. We then introduce the LSM, our contribution to addressing these gaps.

Solving the Big Five – Variability, Scalability, Capability, Acceleration and Sustainability

Five well-known challenges – variability, scalability, capability, acceleration and sustainability – pose challenges for researchers in school interventions focussed on improving valued student outcomes.

Variability

The first, variability, is inherent in education, at every level; from granular to macro-units of analysis (McNaughton, 2011). Variability in effects of teaching and learning outcomes can be seen within classrooms and between classrooms, within schools and between schools, within and between clusters of school and districts and within and between countries.

There are three major explanations for these phenomena. One is the nature of teaching. Teachers are professionals whose very humanness means that they use their tools and deploy instruction in ways that reflect aspects of their knowledge, skills, values and goals. There is plenty of room in what constitutes this personal professionalism for there to be idiosyncratic actions. The second explanation focuses on the degree of specification or prescription in the worlds of teaching: in curricula, syllabi, lesson plans and programmes or in the degree of professional accountabilities either professional or external. The third is the resourcing of teaching such as physical or social resources, the leadership available and how these impact on individual or collective preparation and delivery of instruction. We will have more to say later in this book about these sources of variability, where we address the paradox that variability is both a boon to, and a constraint on effective school change.

A form of variability occurs in programmes or interventions that go beyond a first experimental demonstration. It occurs as the designers, or those tasked with implementing, take what has been demonstrated to be effective to a larger scale. Scalability, that is repeating known-to-be effective instruction across multiple sites, activities and programmes, is a very real problem. The recent evaluation of Reading Recovery in the USA shows this starkly (May et al., 2014). Reading Recovery sets a 'gold standard' for early intervention in literacy. It has been shown repeatedly to be effective for a large percentage of the target children and provides a 'Response to Intervention' means for identifying those for whom a more clinical intensive intervention is needed. Despite an overall strong effect size for Reading Recovery on a variety of outcome measures, the variation in the effect size from school site to school site is substantial. It ranges from a negative effect size, meaning the Reading Recovery intervention children in that site actually got worse than their control group peers, to effect sizes greater than 2.0, almost unheard of in social science research interventions.

Reading Recovery is an exception to the general picture of educational interventions, in the sense that it consistently produces high average or median effect sizes, as well as having this substantial variation. Many experimentally tested programmes in education only ever show weak or small effects when implemented across groups of schools. For example, in the USA since the Education Science Reform act in 2002, the Institute of Educational Sciences has funded about 90 methodologically strong randomised control trials (RCTs), 9 out of 10 of which (88%) found no or weak effects (Coalition for Evidence-Based Policy, 2013).

There are methodological reasons why few show important educational effects (see Schochet, Puma, & Deke, 2014). One of the most obvious of the problems is integrity in implementation. Programmes are hard to put in place reliably if the criterion is being consistent with the original programme design. Durlak and DuPre (2008) recently reviewed 500 health and education programmes for children and adolescents in studies from 1976 to 2006. There were generally low levels of compliance to the programme design.

Each person who is directly responsible for the intervention on the ground is a source of variability, and weakness in implementation. This is true in Reading Recovery where being able to use the complex assessment and instructional procedures flexibly and adaptively for each child can be difficult. In addition, there are features of context across the different sites of an intervention, which may be influential. Durlak and DuPre (2008) identified 23 contextual factors that influence implementation. These include differences from the initial experimental site that change the implementation needs; these could be in the characteristics of teachers and students, such as language or knowledge. There can be differences between the original demonstrations that occur under carefully controlled and well-resourced conditions with the more open complex conditions that typically operate which may be less well funded. In the case of Reading Recovery, advocacy by a principal and the status accorded the intervention in a school, as well as resourcing in terms of time and funding at a district level are influential.

Scalability

Scalability is a form of replication; in Murray Sidman's (1960) terms it is 'systematic replication'. In educational settings it is impossible to have as it were a true replication ('direct replication') – that is, repeating the same experiment in exactly the same way under exactly the same conditions. Schools are not laboratories and except under very special circumstances cannot be controlled to make each look like the other for replication purposes. So each step in scaling an intervention should be considered a systematic replication, does it work under these new conditions, with these new groups of teachers and students across these sites that are known to vary in systematic ways (McNaughton, Lai, & Hsiao, 2012).

The finding, that integrity in the 'treatment' design is often compromised, due to methodological and contextual issues on the one hand, and variability in how professionals carry out the intervention on the other, is well established

(Schochet et al., 2014). The old adage applies: 'there is many a slip twixt the cup and the lip'; the distance between what an intervention was designed to do and what it might actually do on the ground and across several grounds is fraught with obstacles.

Capability

The role of leaders and teachers in the aforementioned 'slippage' introduces the third big challenge: it is building capability on the ground to engage in the core activities specified by the evidence-informed design of an intervention. Here is the nub of this challenge, what should be specified? One approach to variability and scalability is to increase treatment integrity, focussing on the specificity of the design or programme itself. The clearer the specification, the more the integrity. Teachers are both human actors and professionals, with all that entails in terms of knowledge, skills, values and beliefs (McNaughton, 2018). This means that they interpret and reconstruct new ideas, new programmes, new methods and new designs through their existing human and professional roles. The more prescribed the actions, the more likely the actions are to be carried out in keeping with the original design features.

Two aspects of this assumption pose problems for research that is able to change practices on the ground. One is in how teachers are positioned and enabled to act. Increased specification to increase adherence to a programme results in teachers being used as technical experts, technicians who follow the prescribed steps. But this is not how teachers of the twenty-first century should be positioned according to Linda Darling-Hammond and John Bransford (2005). For these and other writers teachers need to be more like adaptive experts. More like a Reading Recovery teacher who is flexibly and adaptively able to tailor instruction to the needs of individual learners. Their bespoke instructional designs draw on rich, evidence-informed judgments and an articulated knowledge base of content, learning and instruction. Prescription also does not work well in a context of the increasing diversity in classrooms in many countries, and is less useful in developing the complex repertoire of skills and knowledge needed for life and work leaving school in the twenty-first century, let alone the design skills needed to effectively use digital tools across curricula.

An alternative view of teachers might lead to an approach that favours loose specification. When an intervention comes to town the focus should be on developing teachers' and leaders' understanding of the underlying principles of the design. This might position teachers as more like adaptive experts, but it carries problems too. The looser the specification the more room there is for interpretation and idiosyncratic enacting; much of which may not add value to the original design leading to greater variability and the challenges of taking to scale we have already identified. A different approach, which we explore in this book, is to reconsider the nature of capability. It is not only a capability to carry out an instructional design. In essence, it is the capability to be a co-design expert, in partnership with others including the research partners.

Acceleration

The focus of the developing co-design expertise is most often the improvement of valued student outcomes. That is, learning that is valued by all partners in an educational site. This is not only valued student achievement outcomes, but those sets of skills and knowledge valued across cognitive and social and emotional domains. In the case of achievement the challenge is often to not just improve overall levels, say in mathematics or in literacy for the 'average' student. With students from communities traditionally not well served by schools the challenge is to produce accelerated learning such that all students and not just some subgroups make more than the expected rates of gain. The accelerated learning needs to shift distributions of achievement for students resulting in the entire distribution of interest approximating the national expected distribution.

This fourth challenge is in part because of the problem that school interventions are often tasked to solve: to address long-standing inequalities in achievement at scale. Existing research shows how difficult this task is. Gains through interventions are typically small and need to be accumulated over long periods of time (e.g. Borman, 2005). If a group is on average two years behind where they would be expected to be nationally, a not uncommon finding for some groups of students, making even expected gains is not good enough. Students need to make more than just an expected rate of gain. This is a known problem recognised by the designer of a successful literacy intervention, Reading Recovery. Clay's (2013) developmental argument was that in order for an early intervention programme to be functional for an individual, it needed to change the rate of acquisition to a rate of progress faster than the cohort to whom the individual belonged. This was needed so that over the brief but intensive period of the individualised intervention a learner would come to function within the average bands required for their classroom.

The issue for students from social and cultural groups who have not been well served by school is not the same as in Reading Recovery in that the target is not for a group of students to come to function as a group within average bands. Rather, in the ideal case the distribution of students needs to approximate an expected distribution, in our case of New Zealand (NZ) students, the NZ national distribution. The probability of being in the lower (or indeed the upper) 'tail' of the distribution should be no more or no less than what would be expected for the population as a whole.

There is an added problem facing school interventions that are designed over several years to produce accelerated gains in achievement. It is the presence of summer effects where there is differential growth in learning over the months when schools are closed (Cooper, Charlton, Valentine, & Muhlenbruck, 2000). Students from poorer communities and minority students make less growth than other students over this period contributing to a widening gap in achievement. The challenge is to design powerful school effects that over time are greater than these summer effects. This is an added challenge to meeting the criteria of effective acceleration.

Sustainability

The final big challenge is the issue of sustainability. The field of educational interventions is littered with examples of interventions that were not sustainable (Coburn, 2003). The usual meaning of sustainability is that the programme or design continues to be effective, after the point at which the original intervention conditions have stopped. Does the intervention continue in the school or schools over time, with new teachers and leaders and with new cohorts of students whose demographic characteristics might also be changing? The answer to that question is not unlike the answer to the question of scalability: not necessarily or consistently.

Identifying when an intervention is 'finished' can be problematic in itself (see Chapter Six), but the idea is that evaluation periods, and the specified time over which professional learning and development (PLD) has put the intervention 'in place', define the beginning and end. Although, in the case of interventions such as Reading Recovery or another well-known intervention, 'Success for All', the intervention never really ceases because the intervention is systemic. It includes an infrastructure of more expert personnel who have continuous contact with the teachers and leaders on the ground providing ongoing refreshing of the original programme and integrity to its specifications.

There is form of sustainability that is even more challenging. It is the idea that interventions ultimately are designed to change what, and possibly even how, students learn *over time*. Early intervention in the life course of a student is often seen as the most cost effective form of an educational change, early means the changes are put in place and will sustain. Yet much about what we know in education tells us that early interventions in and of themselves often have weakening effects over time and even then any lasting effects are very dependent on conditions that learners subsequently encounter (McNaughton, 2011).

This is a problem of proximal and distal causation or chains of causation. That is, whether the learner from an early intervention continues to progress appropriately depends on the teaching they then subsequently receive. It also depends on what they have learned and how that enables (or does not enable) their learning to be developmentally sustained. This is not a trivial concern. There are examples where a very powerful intervention at early grade levels has little effect on the learning at later grades, because what is learned and how it has been learned are not developmentally progressive (McNaughton, 2011).

To summarise: the big question we address in this book is how to design research which addresses five seemingly intractable educational challenges. This was a question we faced locally, but the answers to which potentially have global significance. Are there good models for conducting research that achieve these ambitious educational aims? Can they at the same time make important contributions to our theoretical knowledge which are generalisable across contexts?

A New Approach

For a number of years Catherine Snow, a distinguished past President of the American Educational Research Association has questioned the relevance of educational research. One of her key arguments has been that the low status of educational research is in part due to the perceived irrelevance of educational research to practice (Snow, 2016). She proposes various reasons for this, ranging from issues of 'translation' to the reward structures of academia. Education research is perceived as of limited relevance because it is difficult to translate research into practice. It is hard for practitioners – those actively engaged in the education profession such as teachers, school leaders, teacher aides and the like – to access quality research and then transfer what is read to their own context to improve practice (Snow, 2015). There is also what has traditionally been the applied/basic research divide, where applied research, typically conducted in the 'messy' environments of practice, is accorded a lower status and attracts fewer institutional 'rewards' (e.g. tenure) than more basic research, typically controlled trials in labs outside of schools or under tightly controlled conditions within schools (Snow, 2015, 2016).

These problems exist because the twin objectives of educational research – the improvement of practice and the advancement of research knowledge – can be in conflict. Applied research is often perceived as less rigorous, and emphasising the improvement of practice can distract from generating rigorously tested scientific knowledge. But basic research may be perceived as lacking in relevance by the users of the research and puts researchers into the position of controlling knowledge, and schools/teachers into being implementers of that research knowledge (rather than as those with knowledge to contribute).

There are approaches which solve these binaries. Building on early approaches such as those by Ann Brown (1992), three of the more prominent contemporary approaches are: practice-embedded educational research (PEER) promoted by the Strategic Education Research Partnership (SERP) (Snow, 2015), improvement science (Bryk, Gomez, Grunow, & LeMahieu, 2015) and design-based research (DBR) (Design-based Research Collective, 2003). Other similar approaches include continuous improvement models, design studies, design experiments and educational design research (see an extensive list in van den Akker, Gravemeijer, McKenney, & Nieveen, 2006). Although these approaches vary in emphasis, they share many commonalities. They each propose embedding research in problems of practice, building and sustaining research-practice partnerships, attending to both innovations and their implementation and the use of mixed methods involving rigorous, multiple iterations using data (e.g. Anderson & Shattuck, 2012; Bryk et al., 2015; Snow, 2015). At their core is an approach to educational research that potentially overcomes the binaries and achieves both relevance and robustness, one that is embedded in practice, responsive to context and in partnership with practice. The approach is encapsulated in this quote:

> Educational progress is most likely to emerge from approaches to research that create an equal footing for practitioners and researchers, recognising that though these groups accumulate and curate knowledge in different ways, they both have a role in creating tools that can be used to forge lasting improvements. (Snow, 2015, p. 460)

In this book, we will use the terms 'practice-embedded research approaches' or 'research embedded in practice' to refer to the suite of approaches that have the aforementioned common characteristics. But we will use specific names (e.g. DBR) when referring to a specific approach.

Compelling Reasons for Having Research Embedded in Practice

Four rationales help to explain just how the new approaches might be able to address the seeming conflicts between the twin objectives.

'Real-World' Impact

Research that is embedded in practice has the potential to have a greater 'real-world' impact by contributing to solving pressing school problems. There are many examples of this in the literature including the work undertaken by SERP (e.g. National Research Council, 2003), the Middle School Mathematics and the Institutional Setting of Teaching (MIST) (e.g. Cobb, Jackson, Smith, Sorum, & Henrik, 2013), and Bryk and his colleagues' work, most recently with the Carnegie Foundation (e.g. Bryk et al., 2015). In these cases, researchers working with practitioners have solved problems of teaching and learning in mathematics, reading and the like (see Snow, 2015, for examples). Solving these problems in situ, however, can contribute to addressing long-standing societal problems.

One of the most intractable of these, which has profound personal and social costs, is the gap in achievement between linguistically and ethnically diverse students from low socio-economic communities and other students in higher socio-economic communities (e.g. Nair, Smart, & Smyth, 2007). If these approaches, including the LSM described in this book, can address such achievement gaps, replicated over time and contexts in ways that meet the five challenges, then a major and substantial contribution to educational science will be made. Indeed, there is promising evidence that these new approaches can make such a contribution (e.g. Lai & McNaughton, 2016; McNaughton et al., 2012).

The reasons that practice-embedded research approaches and its variants are likely to impact on the real world are intuitively obvious. They are deliberately designed to have 'real-world' impact in a local context. They are not designed out of site and without the local context in mind. This focus makes it more likely that school leaders and teachers support, engage with and implement such research, thereby contributing to its success. But this seemingly obvious point raises complexities about the nature of a context, the nature of generalisable solutions, and knowing what caused what to happen when there are multiple partners, multiple levels of change and where the intervention looks as though it has been made up on the fly. These complexities will be discussed in the following chapters.

Increases Utilisation of Research by Practitioners

Practice-embedded research approaches increase the likelihood that practitioners support, engage with and utilise research knowledge, which in turn addresses the well-documented research-practice gap (Snow, 2015). Research created from and created to be implemented in the local context is more likely to be utilised by practitioners, firstly because there is less 'translation' required between the research and the context of practice. By contrast, more generalised research knowledge and practice may be hard for practitioners to 'translate' to their individual context, as practitioners may not have sufficient expertise or time to turn that knowledge into practices that fit their unique context. Research derived from the practitioner's own setting is also likely to be perceived to be more relevant to their practice, as it is more likely to take into account the constraints of the local context (Robinson & Lai, 2006). Because the local context is respected, there is greater (and less superficial) engagement with the research by practitioners (Robinson & Lai, 2006).

Develops Research Knowledge That Cannot Be Gained in Controlled Settings

Research embedded in practice advances research knowledge on the improvement of practice that could not be gained under controlled experimental conditions. It reveals, for example, the conditions under which an intervention is most effective, the constraints on the success of the intervention and the like (Bryk et al., 2015). This is not to create a false binary between research done under controlled experimental conditions or clinical trials, and practice-embedded research approaches. Rather, they fulfil different functions, which are complementary. Careful clinical trials including RCTs develop precise knowledge of the effectiveness of specific practices and their generalisability under known controlled conditions. However, solving real-world problems in a local context while advancing knowledge requires an additional approach, one that can draw on knowledge from these trials but also knowledge on how these might work in the messy environment of schools, resulting in knowledge building around the conditions under which an intervention is most effective. This is a form of Sidman's (1960) systematic replication.

Addresses and Repositions the Big Five

At the start of this chapter, we posited five well-known challenges for systemic change – variability, scalability, capability, acceleration and sustainability. Practice-embedded research approaches are well positioned to address these. Variability, in all its forms, is not treated as atypical of a research context and a negative feature of schools that must be controlled. Rather it is treated as typical and used to design and implement the intervention. This in turn, not only improves the intervention, but enables it to be scalable or replicable. In the work in Chile, for example, Treviño and his colleagues found that experimental control trials that did not take into account the context and variability across contexts did not produce improvements in school practices and valued student outcomes. Rather, it was when the interventions were designed to be responsive using continuous improvement models that improvements were found (Treviño, Cortázar, & Godoy, 2018). As Bryk et al. (2015) puts it:

> Achieving improvements at scale … is about getting quality results under a variety of conditions. Understanding the sources of variation in outcomes and responding effectively to them is at the heart of quality improvement. (p. 35)

Practice-embedded research approaches also position schools' (i.e. teachers and school leaders) capability differently. Rather than the capability to enact a design, it is about the capability to co-design in partnership with others, including researchers. Rather than focus on issues of school fidelity to a pre-designed intervention, which we argued earlier is fraught, it is about how to build capability for co-designing with integrity to the process as well as the products of that co-design. Capability is built in schools through the design. The result of strengthening the capability of schools through co-design and capitalising on variability is more likely to address the acceleration issues facing researchers and schools at scale. There are enough demonstrations now of this to know these approaches can deliver this capability (e.g. Treviño et al., 2018).

Finally, given the focus on capability with processes, captured in the idea of continuous improvement, sustainability is planned for differently. In practice-embedded research approaches, sustainability becomes a matter of enabling continued improvements in valued student outcomes and further problem solving and not just the continuation of existing intervention practices (We discuss the definition more in Chapter Six).

Sustainability in improved outcomes, let alone sustainability of the processes of problem solving, is difficult to achieve. A best evidence synthesis by Timperley, Wilson, Barrar, and Fung (2007) found only seven studies that showed continued improvements in student achievement after the end of the school PLD programmes and interventions. Again, we are more optimistic now about sustainability given the emerging evidence of the practice-embedded research approaches including our own (Lai, McNaughton, & Hsiao, 2011).

Our Contribution

While there already exists well-argued reasons for changing the way researchers and schools collaborate to achieve their goals, and an increasing number of empirical studies that demonstrate the success of approaches which do this, there are three promising avenues for further research that would be profitable, and where this book can best make a contribution.

Evidence from a Variety of Educational and Policy Contexts

The first contribution is through an examination of the role of context, consistent with the aim to understand the conditions for effectiveness. The application of the

LSM across contexts has thrown into relief commonalities and differences in the fit for purpose solutions and has helped us test the generalisability of solutions.

Understanding applications in contexts beyond the USA where much of the seminal work is located, particularly in our case in a high trust, relatively autonomous school system with limited centralised control, adds to our collective understanding of contexts in terms of constraints and enablers. A critical point here is that testing applications in specific contexts does not mean that the work is only generalisable to like contexts, particularly if we are able to explain the influential properties of the contexts. There are many aspects of the LSM approach that are generalisable and have been used effectively in a range of countries and contexts, adding to the evidence for the generalisability of the approaches. One example is our use of professional learning communities (PLCs) which is akin to networked communities in the USA (Bryk et al., 2015) and Data Teams in the Netherlands (Schildkamp, Poortman, & Handelzalts, 2016). Given we have also repeated applications in other countries and educational contexts which are more hierarchical and lower trust and have less teacher autonomy, in essence we have tested the scalability of the approach. In this book, we discuss and demonstrate how a design-based research-practice partnership can adapt to such local variations while demonstrating integrity to the overall practice-embedded co-design. In this sense, the model we describe in this book is influenced by context, but is not bound to it.

Training of Researchers in Research-Practice Partnerships

Currently few universities focus on training researchers to develop the kinds of research-practice partnerships required by practice-embedded-type approaches and there is a perception that practice-embedded research means the absence of rigour and a paucity of theory (Snow, 2016). What is important is the development of pragmatic, principled and theory-informed approaches to partnerships. An explicit theoretical basis for the partnerships and rigorous ways of testing the partnerships are needed. However, the nature and shape of partnerships are constrained by the context which means that training of researchers to develop and engage with partnerships is optimal when it is context embedded. The training needs to be such that repeated and varied applications informed by theory enable the abstraction of generalisable principles. Thus the training needs to have features of a guild or apprenticeship. To do so requires pragmatic, principled and theory-informed resources on how to do this task in situ, to demonstrate how the context and methodology interact, which is what this book aims to do.

The Improvement of Valued Student Outcomes

Despite reports of larger scale and sustained improvements for different variations of practice-embedded research approaches (see Snow, 2015), their impact is still judged as 'sparse and focussed on a narrow range of outcomes' (Coburn & Penuel, 2016, p. 48). Specifically in DBR, a variation of the wider practice-embedded research approaches described earlier, such success has not yet been achieved at scale. Anderson and Shattuck's (2012) review of a decade of progress in DBR reported that improvements to practice were at the level of small-scale interventions, with no major 'disruptive' shifts to the educational landscape, and that only 66% of the 47 studies on DBR included in their review reported empirical evidence and results of DBR-based research studies. Not surprisingly, they and others propose a research agenda focussed on the process and outcomes to test the assumed benefits of such partnerships (Coburn & Penuel, 2016). Here we describe the results of more than a decade of applications of our design-based research-practice partnership to solving acceleration in student learning.

The Learning Schools Model

The LSM involves researchers and practitioners working in partnership to co-design rigorous research and development to solve shared and urgent problems of practice. The goal is overcoming the five big challenges and in so doing advances research knowledge. The LSM's theoretical and methodological foundations are primarily in DBR (e.g. Anderson & Shattuck, 2012), although it also draws on improvement science (Bryk et al., 2015). Consistent with DBR, it has the twin pursuits of advancing research knowledge and solving urgent problems of practice, involves partnerships between researchers and practitioners, is situated in an educational context, uses mixed methods and focuses on multiple iterations of design and testing (Anderson & Shattuck, 2012). It also draws on improvement science in its focus on accelerating learning through networks of PLCs and has a focus on variation in performance (Bryk et al., 2015). As such, we call our approach a 'design-based research-practice partnership' as it draws from various practice-embedded research approaches. We have called our approach a 'model' rather than a programme to shift the emphasis away from a prescriptive and programmatic view of school reform; neither of which are representative of DBR and its variants. The design focus of the LSM to date has been on improving teaching and school practices to improve valued student outcomes.

In our book, we use the term 'application' of the model when describing the general features of the model that are applicable to all contexts, and when referring to applications of the model across multiple contexts. We use the term 'intervention' when referring to a specific application with an intervention focus in a specific context.

The model is applied in a fixed sequence typically involving three phases. These phases, often a year long, establish and then add to processes in iterative cycles. Represented in design terms the phases look like this: A (Phase 1), A+B (Phase 2), A+B+C (Phase 3).

Phase 1 – Profiling: Phase 1 builds the principles and protocols of the partnership between researchers and educators and their communities through coming to a shared analysis of the problem. The term 'problem' when used in the LSM refers to a situation that requires a solution (Robinson & Lai, 2006), and this framing is neutral, rather than negative. A problem in the LSM in its most generic form is one of being more effective. Phase 1 establishes PLCs and networks of PLCs on site. This is to build distributed capability to analyse data to develop and test hypotheses about the nature of the problem, which in many applications is in aspects of students learning and achievement, and to develop teaching and school practices in line with these hypotheses. By data, we mean, information that is systematically collected and organised (Lai & Schildkamp, 2013) to represent some aspect of the presenting problem. This definition allows for the multiple kinds of data that teachers and school leaders need for decision-making and is deliberately broad to include any relevant information about students, parents, schools and teachers derived from both qualitative (e.g. structured teacher reflections on classroom teaching) and quantitative (e.g. standardised tests) methods of analysis (Lai & Schildkamp, 2013). An outcome of this phase is an agreed focus, which reflects hypotheses about the most reasonable solutions to the problem.

Phase 2 – Resourcing: Phase 2 continues the collaborative analyses and refining of the problem and possible solutions through the data processes. What is added is resourcing to solve the problem identified through profiling. Resourcing includes all actions taken to build on strengths and to address identified needs. The most common form of resourcing in the LSM has been the provision of teacher and leader PLD opportunities designed to build on identified strengths and address identified gaps in instruction and leadership. But resourcing is not limited to PLD and could also include provision of specialist staff, the development of new infrastructure (such as IT infrastructure), the development of texts or other learning resources or family engagement. Feedback loops through the PLCs collaboratively analysing the data established in Phase 1 continue to be critical in the ongoing development of solutions to meet needs. That is why, in design terms, Phase 2 is considered an A+B design, as the collaborative analysis of data (A) continues, but resourcing (B) is added.

Phase 3 – Sustainability: Phase 3 continues the collaborative analysis of data and problem-solving processes established in the prior phases and the resourcing for solutions but adds a collective focus on sustainability. That is why, in design terms, Phase 3 is considered an A+B+C design, as the collaborative analysis of data and resourcing continues but a focus on sustainability (C) is added. This focus functions to embed the processes and the solutions. This takes several forms but is based on continued practice and increased expertise in collecting and analysing data. It might also include planned data-based and teacher-led inquiry projects looking at the solutions within their classrooms, and mini conferences where results and reflections are shared across multiple schools in networks of PLCs. It is often the case that an outcome of this phase is the identification of a new problem and a new cycle of phases begins to be established.

Each phase often lasts a school year or longer depending on the nature of the problem. Each phase informs the subsequent phase, and collaborative analysis of data collected in that phase is used to adjust the design of the subsequent phase. We have found that the profiling phase is critical to the other phases and has typically an immediate discernible effect on the problem (see, e.g., (Lai, McNaughton, Amituanai-Toloa, Turner, & Hsiao, 2009; Lai, Wilson, McNaughton, & Hsiao, 2014)). The model is expressed visually in Fig. 1.

How our model can contribute to improving educational practice and student achievement while advancing research knowledge is discussed more fully in the final chapter of this book. Given the shared problem has been some form of

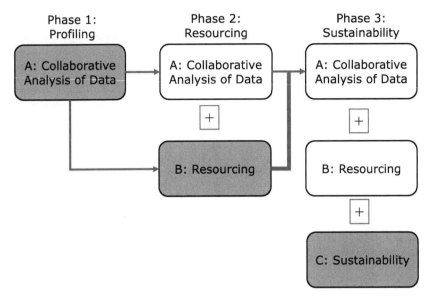

Fig. 1.   The Learning Schools Model Design.

student achievement, we can show that implementing our model has been associated with replicable and consistent accelerations in achievement. These have been in reading, writing and secondary school qualifications and in digital and non-digital contexts; the consequence being reduced disparities for indigenous and ethnic minority students from low socio-economic communities (see summaries in Lai & McNaughton, 2016; McNaughton et al., 2012; and individual studies in, for example, Jesson, McNaughton, Wilson, Zhu, & Cockle, 2018; Lai, McNaughton, Amituanai-Toloa et al., 2009; Lai et al., 2014; Williamson & Jesson, 2017). For example, by the end of one intervention, indigenous students' attainment of the minimum secondary school achievement qualifications was higher than indigenous students' attainment of the certificate nationally, and similar to all students nationally (Lai et al., 2014). In that study, accelerated gains in achievement were made, where the rates of gain were greater than the expected rates nationally. This was educationally significant, given that indigenous students typically perform less well across a range of achievement measures such as national secondary school qualifications and in international tests. It was also significant given that the rates of gains of similar students are typically insufficient to reach national expectations thereby requiring accelerated rates of gain (Lai, McNaughton, Amituanai-Toloa, et al., 2009).

To date we have shown detectable but smaller effects in mathematics (Jesson, McNaughton, Wilson et al., 2018) and the least effects in early literacy (McNaughton & Lai, 2008). Larger effects have been detected at upper primary (around aged 8 years upwards), middle and secondary school levels (Lai et al., 2014). The LSM has improved achievement across a range of contexts and starting achievement levels. These include: urban and rural settings, indigenous and ethnic minorities and the main ethnic group; and students with low starting achievement levels and students with higher starting achievement levels. The LSM interventions involved multiple schools organised into clusters of schools in a similar geographical area.

Two interventions have been across a district and in one case, across three countries. Innovative quasi-experimental designs have been used to determine improvements where the achievement of intervention students was measured using national and/or standardised tests and compared against projected baselines, national rates of progress and norms, and comparison groups (where possible) (described in Chapter Seven). A variety of qualitative and quantitative approaches, often as part of mixed method design, has been used to demonstrate effects. The latter have included statistical analyses including hierarchical linear modelling, odds ratios and inferential tests for differences, and qualitative case studies and observations. (See individual studies listed earlier for details on the methods.)

The improvements have often been substantial, not only for the local system but in terms of international studies. For example, in one LSM intervention with secondary schools, the estimated levels of improvement in reading comprehension achievement compared with comparison groups over the first two years were 0.5 or greater in effect sizes. These effect sizes were higher than those reported for similar reading comprehension interventions with middle and secondary school students implemented by teachers. For example, Scammacca et al. (2007) report effect sizes below 0.10. Where it has been possible to track achievement of the schools post-intervention, improvements in achievement have been sustained after the LSM intervention, in that the average rate of gain in reading comprehension (analysed using statistical modelling) was the same as during the interventions (Lai et al., 2011; Lai, McNaughton, Timperley, & Hsiao, 2009).

Anderson and Shattuck (2012) criticised the research base on DBR as drawing mainly on small-scale interventions. These sustained improvements in achievement using the LSM demonstrate that is possible to achieve outcomes that are both replicable and scalable with DBR-type approaches. Like other DBR-type approaches the LSM provides researchers with alternatives to RCTs that is both rigorous and yet responsive and in partnership with practice. Our rationale for quasi-experimental methods as they are used within the LSM is elaborated further in the final chapter. Finally, the LSM applications show that it is possible for schools to better serve those students from communities who typically do not achieve as well as others (e.g. Jesson, McNaughton, Wilson et al., 2018; Lai & McNaughton, 2016). We can contribute to solving these seemingly intractable problems in ways that are educationally meaningful, scalable and sustainable.

Chapter Two

The Learning Schools Model (LSM)

The LSM is designed to solve educational problems in situ. Researchers and practitioners work in partnership to co-design research and development that solves shared and urgent problems of practice. As a consequence, research knowledge advances. These are major claims. In this chapter, we explain our thinking which underpins the model. This includes the idea of contextualising effective practice to local contexts through a co-design process. Solutions are developed and located within the local context through collaborative analysis of data in PLCs.

Two case studies are used to illustrate the LSM and its applications across diverse contexts, followed by the rationale for the LSM's fixed sequence and focus. Practice-embedded research approaches like the LSM are grounded in and shaped by practice. This means that the local context influences the research design and implementation considerably. In the final section, we discuss the contextual enablers and constraints that have shaped the design and theoretical tenets of the LSM and discuss how the LSM is informed by context, but not limited to it.

Key Concept 1: Contextualisation of Effective Practice to Local Contexts

Much of the process and the content of the solutions generated through the LSM are contextualised. That is, key design features of the LSM – the process of gathering evidence, the development of reasonable hypotheses about possible solutions and those solutions themselves – are developed and located within the local context. The question is why? Why not just assume that a programme will exist, say in reading comprehension, that will fix a presenting problem of low reading comprehension achievement? The answer to this question is dependent on how context is positioned within a research-practice partnership, as a factor to be controlled or as a source of variation that informs the partnership. In Chapter One, we discussed the importance of context, and here we elaborate, drawing on ecological and socio-cultural theories to explain the LSM approach.

Research-practice Partnerships for School Improvement:
The Learning Schools Model, 17–35
Copyright © 2020 by Mei Kuin Lai, Stuart McNaughton, Rebecca Jesson and Aaron Wilson
Published under exclusive license
doi:10.1108/978-1-78973-571-020201003

Understanding Contexts

Children develop in immediate and more distant ecological systems, starting with the interactions between a significant adult such as the teacher and the child, or a parent and the child, the so-called micro-system (Bronfenbrenner, 1979). This system is embedded in other more encompassing systems, created by the relationship between micro-systems within which the developing child moves. Even wider systems include the local neighbourhood, the worlds of work and more generally the overarching institutional, cultural and societal norms, values and practices. Each of these systems has an interaction with and an impact on the developing child. And each changes over time.

The point of the ecological idea is that to understand how children are developing one cannot just focus on the child alone, or indeed just on what patterns of interaction between a teacher and a child in a classroom might look like. Schools are a discrete but not unconnected part of the wider systems. They are quite special systems, being complex, dynamic and open. They change over time as the participants change, with the introduction of new curricula, artefacts, ideas and tools, or even with overarching norms, values and practices changing. The participants have different and evolving roles, ranging from those of leadership through to how students are positioned and the nature of families and their engagement with schools. These components form complex relationships. Change at the level of students' learning will reflect to some degree these complex relationships including the immediate ones with the teacher. We know the quality of teaching contributes a large proportion of the variance in outcomes for students (Hattie, 2009), but it is not the only influential source, and effective teaching is enabled or constrained by these complex relationships.

Socio-cultural theorising adds additional ideas to the ecological framework. The dynamic micro-system of the teacher and student creates zones for development that reflect how the curriculum is operationalised in a particular context (Valsiner, 2000). The configuration of supports provided within these zones, the scaffolds, are contingent and dynamic. They change over time in response to the pace of learning and to what is being learned. The child's ways of thinking and learning both reflect and are a product of these interactions in the micro-system (Rogoff, 2003). The patterns that take place within classroom activities are internalised by children as models of how to think and learn.

The implication of these ideas is that students learn within curriculum channels. That is, curricula, in broad terms, define the bounds and the direction of travel for the socialisation of valued skills and knowledge through schooling. These channels are enacted at the local level and how students progress through the various subject domains is at least in part determined by these channels and the properties of the supports. Moreover, if teaching is conceived as a form of adaptive expertise (Darling-Hammond & Bransford, 2005; Hatano & Inagaki, 1986), where teachers efficiently and innovatively adjust instruction to fit individual students' needs during and outside of the classroom, then the knowledge and skills of the expert teacher determines moment-by-moment uses of instructional acts such as feedback or the design of activities (Hattie, 2009). As such, teaching is conceived also as an act that both influences and is influenced by context.

Arguably then, each context is a product of unique sets of interactions between the actors and the multiple layers of the context, and these interactions influence any design and implementation of an intervention. Therefore, it is important to understand the context of the research-practice partnerships, even if much is known from research or from practice about similar problems in other contexts. Take for example, the case of reading comprehension. In order to comprehend written text, a reader needs to be able to decode accurately and fluently, to have a wide and appropriate vocabulary, have appropriate and expanding topic and world knowledge, active comprehension strategies and active monitoring and fix-up strategies (Block & Pressley, 2002). Children who make relatively low progress and who struggle to comprehend what they have read may have difficulties in one or more of these areas. Moreover, there are other established factors that impact on reading comprehension that are specific to teaching reading comprehension such as direct and explicit instruction for skills and strategies for comprehension (e.g. Slavin, Cheung, Groff, & Lake, 2008). There are also general pedagogical factors that influence learning such as feedback (Hattie, 2009) and building students' sense of self-efficacy and more general engagement and motivation (Wang & Guthrie, 2004). Low progress could therefore be associated with a variety of teaching and learning needs in one or more of these areas. Given the array of teaching and learning needs, those for students and teachers in any particular context will have a context-specific profile. Thus, while our research-based knowledge means there are well-established relationships, the patterns of these relationships in specific contexts may vary.

Consider a second example. There are generic properties of effective teaching such as well-designed feedback or classroom discourse that extends and elaborates a student's answer to a question (Hattie, 2009; Wilkinson & Son, 2010). Similarly, there are known generic properties of effective learning, including practice with multiple and varied exemplars (Bransford, Brown, & Cocking, 2000) and having self-regulatory strategies (Zimmerman, 2006). But knowledge of how these properties specifically apply in the everyday activities of teachers and students in the local context is needed. To assume, for example, that more informative feedback is what is needed requires some checking of the local patterns of feedback as they occur with specific acts of learning. One can have too much feedback, it can get in the way, it can be mistimed. Or how much and what sort of practice is occurring may vary, not just by subject matter and teacher, but also by ability level. Our instructional tools carry risks (McNaughton, 2018), and just what might be the problem in instruction or learning needs collective knowledge and hypothesis formation and testing as we describe in the next chapter.

Knowing the Problem in Context

These ideas about context lead to an important stance. That is, in order to understand the problem that motivated the research-practice partnership we need a detailed understanding of the nature of the problem within the local context. The original problem described at the start of the partnership may not actually be the problem. In our work, we have often found that the problem that led to the partnership has been defined too broadly, such as improving low achievement or the need for better teaching and learning. Developing a more specific description of the problem, such as quite how low, and for whom achievement is low and in what areas or in what contexts, is one sense in which the original problem may not be the problem.

A more complex version of this issue is an assumption that the presenting problem is the immediate or most important problem to solve. Is this problem the one that when addressed is the most likely to lead to, or contribute most to the valued outcomes? Absenteeism, churn in the teaching staff or even lack of clarity of curriculum expectations and appropriate materials could be more important than the quality of teaching by creating conditions that constrain effective teaching and learning.

It is also possible that there is no actual evidence to support the first assumptions about the problem. We found this in some of our applications of the model, where systematic data collection into the perceived problem revealed the problem to be non-existent or as having little influence on the outcomes of interest as originally thought. Without gathering and interpreting the evidence from the local context such mistakes are easily made. Buly and Valencia (2002) provide a case study of the importance of basing any intervention on specific profiles, rather than making assumptions about what children need (and what instruction should look like). In that study, mandating phonics instruction for all students who fell below literacy proficiency levels in a US state was shown to have missed the needs of the majority of students, whose decoding was strong but who struggled with comprehension or language requirements for the tests. Thus, even the most reasonable hypotheses about the problem and its solutions need to be tested in some way.

However, the point is not whether the original proposed problem is inaccurate or incomplete. It is that evidence needs to be gathered to support, clarify or change what is assumed. The originally proposed problem may turn out to be the agreed problem, and aspects of teaching and learning may very well be limiting achievement. But even so, coming to identify the most likely causal aspects requires local profiles of teaching and learning, and as such, understanding these context-specific profiles are critical.

Why Context Matters to a Partnership

Developing context-specific profiles benefits how teachers act and adopt new practices and innovate. Collecting evidence from a context will reveal examples of practices or individuals who are very effective. Knowing about their effectiveness within the complexities of the local system provides a critical source of evidence of how to be effective within that context and then can be used to develop solutions. The use of this sort of variability or 'positive deviance' is based on the well-founded belief that variability will exist in some parts of system and some of that variability, the positive forms, already have solutions or parts of solutions for existing problems (e.g. McNaughton, 2011). This is a strength-based approach grounded in realistic optimism, and in direct opposition to the view that the system does not have *any* capability to solve the current problem. This does not mean we romanticise the capability of teacher and school community and ignore capability issues in the system. Rather, that we use variability to uncover areas of strength to co-design more effective solutions. Our approach thus acknowledges that there can be effective practices in contexts even where the general practices are weak.

A second benefit of developing context-specific profiles relates to teaching expertise and the role of knowing about one's actions, either those as an individual, or as part of a community. The more that positive outcomes are seen to be closely related to individual action (self-efficacy) or collective actions (collective efficacy), the more they are effective in changing beliefs and behaviour (Bandura, 1995). Strong collective efficacy is a predictor of student achievement at a school level (Bandura, 1995). A wide spread sense of efficacy also supports the further development of personal efficacy, the latter being associated with an increased commitment to teaching and innovating, and greater resilience in the face of difficulties (McNaughton, 2002). Identifying positive variations in practice through context-specific profiles can build collective and individual efficacy, as teachers in the community see instances where their colleagues or a set of practices have been effective under similar circumstances. Such evidence demonstrates the possibilities for improvement in seemingly intractable circumstances.

The third benefit of the profile relates to the known difficulties of changing core teacher practices and sustaining those changes. One reason for such difficulties is that the interventions and/or PLD experiences do not provide detailed and authentic experiences that make sense to teachers, and thus are not fully adopted by teachers (Timperley, 2011). Evidence from the local context can offer more powerful ways for teachers to embed and sustain changes, as these changes are developed within the local context. For example, PLD approaches in which teachers try to solve a problem in their own context have been found to be more effective than those that are decontextualised from practice such as one off workshops (see seminal review by Hawley & Valli, 1999, and best evidence synthesis by Timperley et al., 2007).

Going Beyond the Local

In Chapter One, we claimed that the LSM like other DBR-type approaches can contribute to our scientific knowledge. The contextualising that is fundamental to the LSM does not mean general principles cannot be extracted or that new knowledge cannot be developed, for example, about the nature of teaching and learning or about schools as systems. In fact, we believe this should be a core commitment of research approaches like the LSM. Despite treating each context as relatively unique in the first instance, effective designs which are tested can contribute to the storehouse of scientific knowledge. We show how in Chapter Seven.

Before concluding this section, it is worth mentioning that the contextualisation is generally of effective *practice*, and not of an effective *programme*. That is, we do not take a known programme such as Reading Recovery, and put that into place before the partnership has come to a shared understanding of the evidence from the local contexts. The goal of the partnership is to be more bespoke, in terms of putting together elements of effective practice that could exist in one or across several evidence-informed programmes to address what is the best set of hypotheses from the local context.

Key Concept 2: Collaborative Analysis of Data

In the LSM, collaborative analysis of data plays a central role. In design terms, it is the 'A', in the additive and iterative A, A+B, A+B+ design. Why have we foregrounded analysis of data in our design, and why is the focus on collaborative, rather than individual analysis of data? The answer is located firstly in the research tradition of the LSM. While analysing data is fundamental to evaluating most school interventions, in DBR-type approaches, such analyses have an added function. They are the basis for decision-making in the iterative design and redesign process (Anderson & Shattuck, 2012). The LSM follows in this tradition. What is foregrounded in the LSM, however, are additional central functions of collaborative analysis. These multiple functions include to develop context-specific profiles for the co-designing of solutions (Key concept 1), for capability and partnership building, and for sustainability. The rationale for these draws on socio-cultural and socio-cognitive theories, and the empirical literature on previous successes of this approach, as well as the nature of the problem to be solved. But before we describe those, we need to define what we mean by collaborative analysis of data due to the competing agendas associated with this term.

Understanding Collaborative Analysis of Data

Our approach to collaborative analysis of data is aligned with the NZ curriculum, that is, 'Since any teaching strategy works differently in different contexts for different students, effective pedagogy requires that teachers inquire into the impact of their teaching on their students' (Ministry of Education, 2007, p. 35). This curriculum approach is part of the evidence-based teacher inquiry tradition; a tradition which is usually associated with low-stakes formative assessment using a variety of data sources, rather than top-down, externally driven accountability associated with high stakes testing. It eschews inappropriate uses of data such as teaching to the test. The process involves the analysis of multiple sources of data (both qualitative and quantitative) to develop and test hypotheses of the problem, to determine solutions to that problem and to evaluate these solutions.

By 'collaborative', we mean that such analysis is undertaken in PLCs that critically interrogate their own practices in an ongoing, reflective, collaborative, inclusive, learning-oriented, growth-promoting way (Toole & Seashore-Louis, 2002) to improve student learning. The focus on student learning is foregrounded in these PLCs, as without this focus, PLCs can default to entrenching existing practice and the assumptions on which it is based. An older but significant study by Lipman (1997) provides a cautionary case where communities of teachers tasked with developing ways to better integrate African-American students into the school focussed more on difficulties with the students, rather than their own practice. This resulted in the only African-American teacher in the group withdrawing from the group, and nothing changed for the students. Our definition of collaborative analyses of data is also 'critical' in that analysis involves a rigorous examination and evaluation of the data using appropriate evaluation criteria, as opposed to a discussion of 'good ideas' which are not evaluated. Under our definition of PLCs, such communities can be within and across schools, can involve participants outside of a school such as researchers, and can include networks of such communities (often defined as professional learning networks, Brown & Poortman, 2018). In the LSM, these PLCs typically comprise configurations of researchers, teachers and school leaders.

The hypothesised mechanisms for learning through collaborative analysis of data in a PLC draw on both socio-cultural and socio-cognitive theories, which argue that knowledge is constructed through interactions with others, and learning occurs in interactions. Learning is enhanced through the shared cognition developed in the PLC (Wenger, 1998), in other words, enhanced through social interactions with others who bring different types and forms of knowledge to achieve similar goals. The knowledge from the PLC to address these goals can be in the form of complementary knowledge, where each community member draws on a different knowledge base to develop and critique both new and existing practices to understand and solve a common problem (Earl & Timperley, 2008). PLCs also offer the opportunity to learn from others who might have greater knowledge and skills in solving the problem under consideration.

The need to learn from others is foregrounded in the LSM because the knowledge required to solve deep pedagogical challenges at the level of classroom practices and school leadership and of the sort the LSM typically deals with is both extensive and intensive. Extensive because the problem that began the partnership is often broad to begin with (e.g. to improve reading comprehension for students from linguistically diverse communities). Extensive also because of the complexity associated with understanding and acting on the problem. Intensive because we need to develop sufficiently fine-grained hypotheses and solutions to address the identified problems (see Chapter Three). In short, we need a large pool of knowledge to draw on and a depth of knowledge to understand the problem and possible solutions. Individual knowledge levels typically need to be augmented to address these problems. Moreover, the problem is located within a context that is a product of interactions across a unique set of actors (teachers, students, etc.) within a larger multi-layered ecological system. Therefore, the knowledge of multiple actors is required to both understand the interactions that produced the problem and the solutions that can work within the context, which may include changing the context or aspects of it.

Given the socially constructed nature of knowledge in a PLC, it is important that the PLC's shared ideas, beliefs and goals are theoretically rich. Theoretically rich knowledge is both knowledge about the target content-area that is the focus of the partnership and a detailed understanding of the nature of teaching and learning related to that content-area. Being theoretically rich requires not just consideration of research theories but the engagement of practitioners' tacit ones (Robinson, 1993). Engaging the practitioners' theories uncovers the reasons and conditions that have resulted in their current practices. This allows others in the PLC to challenge the reasons, if, for example, they are based on inaccurate assumptions, and understand the necessary conditions that need to be taken into account to improve practice. This process of considering both practitioner and research theories is important for developing evidence-based context-specific profiles. For example, it surfaces knowledge about the context which the researchers may not be privy to, thus increasing the likelihood of developing a well-matched context-specific profile. It serves to increase teacher motivation to engage with the research, as it demonstrates respect for practitioner knowledge.

Not only do practitioners' theories need be engaged alongside researchers' theories, but any tensions need be resolved against criteria that do not privilege either theory (Robinson & Lai, 2006). For example, tested against the criteria that each proposed theory has to be supported by evidence. Confirming and disconfirming evidence among partners needs to be treated and tested equally. In this way, both sources of knowledge (practice and research) are seen as important without an uncritical and untested acceptance of knowledge of either source. This is the basis for addressing a potential weakness in partnerships raised by Snow (2015), namely that the PLCs need to distinguish between 'insightful teacher tips and effective invented practices from their opposite' (p. 464). Having agreed protocols for gathering and using the evidence in the PLCs provides a way of testing teachers tips and practices that is both shared but rigorous. Our approach is therefore in contrast to research-practice partnerships focussed on the 'buy-in' to an approach (e.g. whether sufficient teachers support the reform before it is embedded) and is more than just using practice knowledge to develop effective practices that researchers can incorporate into their intervention design.

The inclusion and testing of both researcher and practice knowledge in the collaborative process has further advantages. Teachers, leaders and researchers are also members of other communities beyond the school or the research institution. An overly insular PLC based just on the researchers or the schools runs the risk of functioning in a silo (Tett, 2015) and can have limited 'horizons of observation' (Little, 2003, p. 917); that is the more homogeneous the community, the more it is limited by its preconceptions and limited in the solutions it can develop. Collaborations that include others beyond the usual horizon of observation can increase the knowledge base and provide new perspectives that can enhance the analysis process.

Data and Data Literacy Skills

Although we have presented the two key concepts separately, they work in concert in the LSM. The contextualisation of effective practice to local contexts requires the collection, analysis and understanding of local evidence, and this is enacted through the collaborative analysis of data processes in our research design. The collaborations strengthen and augment the contextualisation efforts resulting in profiles that are both content and context specific. Thus, the two concepts not only work in tandem to develop context-specific profiles for design purposes, but also build capability and develop shared understanding, thereby increasing the likelihood of engagement and also sustainability post-intervention.

Underlying both key concepts is the use of data. What we have described in this chapter is how data are used in order to co-design and in order to function effectively as a PLC. There is considerable evidence that the data use component is very important. The evidence comes from reviews of professional development (e.g. Hawley & Valli, 1999; Timperley et al., 2007), reviews of effective PLCs (e.g. Vescio, Ross, & Adams, 2007) and large-scale randomised trials of interventions that have data use as a component (e.g. Carlson, Borman, & Robinson, 2011; Taylor, Pearson, Peterson, & Rodriguez, 2005). However, results from studies of data use in PLCs, in interventions, and/or through PLD are variable, as judged by student outcomes (Lai & McNaughton, 2016). We see data use as a necessary but insufficient condition for effective partnerships. Other facets of PLCs and more broadly partnerships are at play, which determine effects.

It is also clear that the skills needed to enact key concept 1 and key concept 2 are complex, and they are skills not necessarily part of the usual set that a teacher, school leader or researcher might have. These skills are firstly data literacy skills, which are commonly interpreted as the collection, examination, analysis and interpretation of data to inform some sort of decision in education settings (Gummer & Mandinach, 2015). Such skills are not typically part of teacher training college curricula (Gummer & Mandinach, 2015), and there is general agreement that teachers need support to develop the knowledge and skills required to use data for decision-making (e.g. Schildkamp & Kuiper, 2010).

There are also cognitive and social skills that are interdependent with others, such as being able to see a problem differently, to adopt someone else's perspective, to be amenable to being wrong or less skilled than one thought. Whitty (2008) sees these sets of skills as new forms of professionalisation; they constitute 'collaborative professionalism' and he and others have written extensively about these attributes required of teachers in schools (Fullan, Rincon-Gallardo, & Hargreaves, 2015). Such skills need to be developed through the LSM, and this is why the first phase is so important.

Two Case Studies

We previously described the LSM as having three additive and iterative phases of fixed sequence using an A (Phase 1), A+B (Phase 2), A+B+C (Phase 3) design, where A is Collaborative analysis of data, B is Resourcing and C is Sustainability. While these phases have a fixed sequence, they can be instantiated differently across contexts due to the differences in context and curriculum needs, and the like. Here, we present two intervention case studies to illustrate the LSM and its applications across diverse contexts.

The first intervention involved seven schools from an urban, low socioeconomic community comprised of primarily indigenous and ethnic minority students from the Pacific nations (Lai, McNaughton, Amituanai-Toloa, et al., 2009). Students in the intervention were 9–11 years old. The second intervention involved seven schools in a rural and small-town region serving primarily indigenous and the majority ethnic group communities, with students ranging from 13 to 15 years old being the focus of the intervention (Lai et al., 2014). Prior to these interventions, the researchers had worked in both communities, in the first case through a related intervention, and in the second case through an LSM intervention with schools with primary aged students in the same community. As such, prior to the intervention commencing, there had been discussions between key partners (schools and in the case of the second intervention, members of a Trust funding the intervention) on the possible problems that might need to be collectively solved. In addition, in both communities there were pre-existing PLCs between and within schools, and these were co-opted for use in the intervention. Both interventions adopted a quasi-experimental design to determine intervention impact, comparing the achievement of intervention students with comparison groups of students and against a baseline of achievement established at the start of the intervention.

In the first intervention, which we will call the 'primary school intervention', the problem was more clearly defined – school leaders wanted to improve achievement in reading comprehension which was much lower than national expectations and they were focussed on improving the quality of instruction in the classroom towards meeting that aim. There were existing data that supported the focus in the form of test scores, and in this sense, the problem to be solved was 'real' and not merely perceived. In the second, which we will call the 'secondary school intervention', there was a mystery to be solved – achievement in the national secondary school qualifications and other assessments were significantly lower than would be expected given reading comprehension achievement in primary schools. In short, there was a developmental disconnect between students' initial high levels of reading comprehension, and subsequent levels of achievement (including reading) over three years at secondary school. In this case, it was less clear what the problem actually was, and where the solution to the problem might lie given the variety of possible hypotheses about the problem ranging from transition to secondary school to students' lack of engagement.

Phase 1: Profiling

A key goal of the profiling phase is to develop an agreed focus that reflects hypotheses about the most reasonable solutions to the problem. This is achieved through collaborative analysis of data to develop and test hypotheses about student learning, and develop teaching and school practices in line with these hypotheses. Through this collaborative analysis process, the principles and protocols of the partnership are established; context-specific profiles are developed to enable the contextualisation of effective practice to local contexts (key concept 1); collective capability in analysing and using data is developed; and the sustainability of the intervention is developed. These collaborations are enacted in PLCs, where the focus is on collaboratively analysing data to develop collective approaches to solve problems of practice.

The starting points for the two interventions were different which meant that the standard profiling process had different intensities and breadth of data collection. In the primary school intervention, the clearly defined problem of improving reading comprehension and improving the quality of instruction meant that the data collection was less extensive, albeit in-depth, with a focus on the reading achievement and the instruction relating to that achievement. Thus, the partners agreed to start the Profiling phase by collecting achievement data in reading comprehension using two standardised tests that were nationally normed, and researchers conducted classroom observations. The former also formed the baseline achievement analysis to measure intervention success at the end of the intervention.

The initial data collection led to a series of collaborative analysis sessions in cluster (across-school) PLCs comprised of school leaders and researchers, and in within-school PLCs comprising all school staff, school leaders and researchers. These meetings focussed on understanding the extent of the achievement problem (e.g. levels of achievement compared to national norms and variability) and the specific strengths and weaknesses in reading comprehension (e.g. vocabulary). The meetings also focussed on understanding how instructional practices in the classroom might be related to these needs, for example, existing instructional practices in vocabulary compared to the students' strengths and weaknesses in vocabulary. These discussions led to co-constructed hypotheses about both the nature of the student strengths and learning needs, and also the instruction in the classroom that could address the needs and build on the existing student strengths. These hypotheses drew on both evidence from practice in the local context and existing research.

In the secondary school intervention, the goal was to understand the developmental disconnect between high literacy levels in the primary school context and subsequent levels of achievement in the secondary school context. Hence, the focus of the profiling was to develop an understanding of what the actual problem was. A wide range of achievement data from the national secondary school qualification assessments and literacy assessments was gathered to understand the extent of the problem, as well as patterns of achievement over time to determine, for example, if there were 'choke points' where achievement started to drop. The achievement data were also used as a baseline to measure intervention success at the end of the intervention. These profiles were then discussed in a series of cluster PLCs and within-school PLCs, where a series of hypotheses about the patterns of achievement were raised; some by school leaders and some by researchers. These hypotheses drew on both evidence from practice in the local context and existing research.

Although there was little literature directly addressing the unusual developmental disconnect and the context of the work, there was related research which could be brought to the specific case. This included data about interference effects of the transition between primary to secondary school; higher achieving students leaving the rural and small-town schools to attend secondary school in larger cities; socialisation effects as students might value education less given full employment in the region at that time; and instructional effects, both general pedagogy, teacher–student relationships and the specific instruction in literacy (see details in Wilson, McNaughton, & Lai, 2011). Data were then collected to test these hypotheses. For example, the numbers and achievement levels of those who did not continue studying in the region compared to those who did.

These data suggested that fewer students left the region than was hypothesised, and that the achievement levels were slightly higher, but not significantly so. As such, the hypothesis that students leaving the schools were responsible for the drop was refuted. Other hypotheses however were confirmed in relation to the low rates of literacy teaching at secondary school, but not general pedagogy or teacher–student relationships.

In both interventions, once the hypotheses were refined to specific practices that were most likely related to the student achievement profiles, the teachers and researchers began co-constructing practices to address these specific practices and schools began to put those into practice through their normal school and classroom routines. For example, in one school in the primary school intervention, the school leader developed an activity to address the identified weakness in instruction and teachers used those where appropriate.

Researchers also used this information to begin to co-design with relevant school leaders how best to address these areas of need through targeted resourcing in Phase 2. In both these interventions, the design of the resources was led by the researchers with school personnel helping to refine the content of the resources, in this case PLD sessions and to plan how best to implement the PLD sessions. Finally, as part of the quasi-experimental design, student achievement data were collected twice a year along with other relevant data for the design (e.g. data on intervention implementation) to evaluate the impact of the Phase 1 activities, and to inform the collaborative analysis of data in Phase 2.

The results of this Phase, as we have found in other LSM studies, resulted in statistically significant and educationally significant improvements in achievement. Thus profiling using collaborative analysis of data is not just a 'pre-intervention activity' to design the subsequent intervention. Rather, profiling can raise achievement. On reflection it is predictable that the profiling phase would begin changes in classrooms, even prior to any specific resources because of the collective problem solving and shared evidence-informed focus.

Phase 2: Resourcing

Phase 2 continues the collaborative analysis and refining of the problem and possible solutions through the data process. What is added is resourcing to build on existing strengths and address identified needs, where resourcing includes all actions taken to build on strengths and address needs identified in the profiling phase, for example, PLD, digital learning objects. Resourcing may include explicit development of knowledge where an expert presents pedagogical content knowledge (PCK) and content knowledge about the content-areas identified as weaknesses in Phase 1 and what the literature argues are effective practices to address them. However, this explicit development of knowledge is always accompanied by collaborative analysis of data where teachers apply their new knowledge by developing practices, test them in their classrooms and discuss their findings with their peers.

In both studies, resourcing in the second phase involved PLD through a series of sessions based on the identified needs. There were some differences in how the school leaders and teachers engaged with the PLD and who attended the PLD based on the logistics of the intervention and the amount of associated research funding. In the primary school intervention, the PLD led by one of us involved 10 sessions with school leaders and teachers and was designed using the profiles and known dimensions of effective teaching. . The curriculum for the sessions used a mixture of theoretical and research-based ideas as well as teacher investigation and exemplification from their own classrooms. There was also a continued focus on collaborative analysis of data, as teachers would apply their knowledge from the session in their classroom by refining their practice and then analysing and reporting on the outcome of their refined practice in the next session using evidence to support their interpretations. For example, one session introduced theories and research relating the role of vocabulary in comprehension. Readings were used such as Biemiller (1999) and Pressley (2000), and those which identified features of effective teaching of vocabulary. The task for this session was to design a simple study carried out in the classroom which looked at building vocabulary through teaching with teachers reporting on the outcome of that in the next session.

The PLD in the secondary school intervention was similarly focussed on the issues identified in the Profiling Phase. Given the generally low rates of literacy instruction in content-areas identified in the profiling and the variability across teachers, it was important to focus first on a core-set of practices in order that students experience more, and more coherent, literacy instruction across content-areas. An initial set of seven 45-minute sessions was prepared by the research team in collaboration with the school leaders focussed on these core practices such as effective literacy instruction (e.g. Shanahan & Shanahan, 2008) and reading instruction (e.g. Palincsar & Brown, 1984). However, the sessions were delivered differently because the schools were spread out geographically, the researchers were not based in the geographical location as the schools, and the funding was low. The sessions were delivered to school leaders who were expected to deliver them to all staff. Each session consisted of a video-taped mini-presentation with accompanying PowerPoint, instructions for the school leader delivering the workshop, practical hands-on activities, suggestions for next steps and further reading. Because of the delivery method and the geographical spread of the schools, the preparation and training for the workshops occurred in a series of seven video conferences. In these sessions, readings were discussed, the collective problem solving of in-school issues occurred and leaders prepared for delivering the specific workshops of PLD with the whole staff. The researchers also checked whether school leaders had delivered the Phase 2 PLD to their teachers as intended by interviewing all relevant school leaders (principals and literacy leaders tasked with leading the intervention in their schools) at the end of Phase 2, and triangulated their responses with anonymous teacher surveys which asked teachers what sessions had been delivered and further information about the delivery (e.g. to whom it had been delivered).

Because of the additive nature of the design, collaborative analysis continued in both interventions with face-to-face PLCs held between two to three times during the year with school leaders. In such PLCs, the collective data discussion process continued from Phase 1, with feedback and discussion of implementation and student outcomes. Because of the delivery method of the secondary school intervention, these collaborative analysis sessions were augmented by support for school leaders to deliver the workshops to staff including training on how to disseminate knowledge to staff and further clarification of workshop knowledge, if necessary. As part of the quasi-experimental design, student achievement data were collected twice a year along with other relevant data for the design (e.g. data on intervention implementation) to evaluate the impact of the Phase 2 activities, and to inform the collaborative analysis of data in Phase 3.

Phase 3: Sustainability

Phase 3 continues the collaborative analysis of data and problem-solving processes established in the prior phases and the resourcing for solutions, but adds a collective focus on sustainability. The focus is designed to deeply embed the processes and solutions, and can take several forms depending on the context and the evidence from the collaborative analysis of data.

Both interventions continued the collaborative analysis of data and resourcing, but there was a stronger focus on sustainability in the primary school intervention. The difference was due to the contexts of the two interventions and the emerging data from Phase 2. In the primary school intervention, the context was an urban, low socio-economic community where there is high teacher turnover and student transience and a long history of academic under-achievement. The secondary school intervention was in the context of a rural and small-town region with less reported teacher turnover and student transience. Moreover, in the secondary school intervention, the data from Phase 2 suggested that achievement gains stalled in the second year and that the resourcing needed augmenting through a focus on content-area literacy if gains were to continue being made. For those two reasons, the secondary school intervention focussed on resourcing around content-area literacy with collaborative analysis of data continuing.

The context and data analysis of the primary school intervention, by contrast, led to a strong focus on sustainability through a separate set of resourcing activities designed to strengthen the collaborative analysis of data, and to develop systems and processes for embedding the resources and the collaborative analysis of data processes into the school's normal routines. The existing collaborative analysis of data in PLCs was extended by having teams of teachers carry out classroom inquiry projects using collaborative analysis of data to support sustainability. Projects were centred on identified achievement issues in teachers' classrooms; these were then presented and discussed in an across-school teacher conference. Examples of inquiry projects include refining instructional strategies to increase the use of complex vocabulary in writing, redesigning homework to raise literacy levels and the teaching and skimming and scanning in reading. Each project involved the use of formal or informal assessments of student outcomes. A total of 11 projects were presented (conference format) at a teacher-led conference in the fourth term of the school year that 90% of the teachers attended. Other professional colleagues such as literacy advisors attended the conference also.

A major new feature was the development and use of planned inductions into the focus and patterns of teaching and professional learning in the schools. The schools experienced staff turnover of differing degrees from year to year but on average around a third of the staff changed from year to year. This component was designed to maintain and build on the focus with new staff. One of us also provided theoretical and content knowledge on effective sustainability practices, for example, by providing and discussing readings relating to sustainability that were relevant to the issues faced by schools. As part of the quasi-experimental design, student achievement data were collected twice a year along with other relevant data for the design (e.g. data on intervention implementation).

Sequence of the Model

The LSM sequence of the phases is prescribed. This prescribed sequence is based on years of testing and of the logic of a DBR research approach. The profiling phase focussed on collaborative analysis of data is always the first phase. As argued in the key concept 1, even though we could develop reasonable hypotheses about possible solutions, these hypotheses and solutions need to be located within a local context. Only by understanding these context-specific profiles can effective resources be developed to target the specific issues that led to the presenting problem. The process of profiling also serves to establish the partnerships through the collaborative use of data to develop and test shared hypotheses in a respectful and rigorous way, and serves as PLD by modelling the process for school partners. Given the key concepts and the underlying logic it does not make any sense to shift the phases around. A fit for purpose set of resources depends on understanding what the context-specific teaching and learning needs are. On the other hand, we can establish the profiling process without full understanding of the practices to be refined or resources to be developed because we assume and treat teachers as adaptive experts with sufficient knowledge to contribute to the collaborative analysis of data. In our work, we have consistently found variability in teacher knowledge sufficient for such analyses, which is then augmented through the collaborative knowledge building in the PLCs.

The LSM could hypothetically continue with collaborative analysis of data without a resourcing phase, if schools have the capacity to do so without researcher input. However, in all our studies, the first phase typically reveals gaps in either theory- or practice-based knowledge that constrains the amount of improvement that can be made by teachers and school leaders, resulting in the profiling stage being used to determine resourcing (Phase 2). This does not imply that the teachers use 'bad' practices. Our studies typically show that teachers by and large are using approaches that might be considered within the range of 'good practice'. Often we also find students in the schools serving diverse low socio-economic communities making expected progress, thereby reflecting the strength of the teaching. However, these generically thought to be effective practices are not sufficient or less effective to solve stubborn issues and accelerate learning; or these practices need to be contextualised better to meet identified student needs. Thus, our emphasis on the importance of knowledge and its foregrounding, as well as the empirical evidence collected over the years, suggest the importance of this second phase. For example, we found in one intervention that achievement gains in Phase 1 plateaued after an initial gain, and it was only when a particular type of resourcing in the form of literacy PLD was added that more sizable gains were made.

The final phase involves a collective focus on sustainability to deeply embed the process and solutions, and is designed to strengthen the practices for sustainability already built into the design in Phases 1 and 2 through the collaborative analysis. A concerted focus on sustainability in preparation for the end of the formal partnership (usually the end of the funding) is both important and necessary. This is because the typical context of our work is in the poorest communities whose educational profiles on entry to school are below expected levels often remain stubbornly static, and where there needs to be sustained improvements in achievement post-intervention.

Again, logically, sustainability is the last phase. This is because we need to know if the intervention has worked as intended and if so, what worked, before we sustain 'it'. In our view, a concerted focus on sustainability has to be warranted, and we would not focus on Phase 3 without evidence that justifies a concerted sustainability focus. The justification comes from the first two previous phases. They have built in mechanisms to check for effectiveness and links between practices and outcomes through the collaborative analysis of data processes and the standard DBR process, typically using a quasi-experimental design, where data are used to check the effectiveness of the intervention and to make adjustments. As such, these other phases come prior to, and become the basis of, the sustainability phase.

The case studies were used to show how, the LSM is instantiated differently across sites due to the differences in context and curriculum needs and foci. They differed in the intensity and breadth of data collection and analysis, and there were differing lengths of time in each phase. But, the sequence remained the same.

The NZ Context and its Affordances

The contexts within which research operates are often invisible drivers of design. In this last section we make transparent the aspects of the NZ educational system that provide both enablers and constraints on the design of our model and how it has been applied in schools. However, while the LSM is influenced by context, it is not bound to it, and the influence of the context and the LSM can be bi-directional. In what follows, we discuss four contextual influencers on the LSM, which is not an exhaustive list, but an indicator of the influence of context.

Firstly, the design of the LSM is predicated on an education system that is in general rated as high quality as per OECD reports, and where teachers have, in general, effective practices, but that these practices needed to be adapted to address needs of culturally and linguistically diverse students. For example, in

OECD tests and in national tests, there are large disparities between the achievement of indigenous Māori and Pacific Islanders and other students, although achievement in general is high (e.g., OECD, 2013). Thus, the design assumes sufficient teacher capacity to contribute to the partnership through the collaborative analysis of data processes.

In education systems where there is less overall teacher capability, the LSM can still be used as there is still likely to be variability on which to capitalise. Some teachers and some schools will have developed demonstrably effective practices. However, some features of the LSM might need to be modified, for example, data can still be used as a tool to develop the partnerships, but there may be more emphasis on addressing misapprehensions of teachers, less reliance on within school processes for sharing ideas, and more emphasis on shared planning by the research team with teachers. In the LSM work in nations with lower overall teacher capability, there has still been joint collaborative analysis of data alongside co-design of teaching responses to students' need. In fact, in such contexts where teachers possibly have a smaller instructional repertoire to draw on to contribute to the partnership, co-design through understanding the relationships between teaching and learning becomes even more important to engage with and support teachers' emerging understandings.

The second feature which has influenced how partnerships are conceived in the LSM is that NZ is a self-governing school system. In this system, state schools are government funded and operated, but they are governed by an elected Board of Trustees comprising of parent trustees, the principal, staff and student-elected trustees (in schools with students above Year 9) and co-opted trustees (Ministry of Education, n.d.-a). The educational system is therefore less organisationally structured than other systems with an emphasis of local accountability through the Boards of Trustee, monitored by a national quality assurance agency, which adopts a negotiated (with schools) and developmental approach to school evaluation (Lai & Kushner, 2013). The NZ school structure gives significant autonomy over educational decisions to local communities and schools, including whether to participate in research, and school partners in this structure are both powerful and agentic.

A constraint which this second feature poses is that schools have tended to function in isolation one from another. While there were some across-school PLCs when we began our work, across- school PLCs where there is sharing of data and resources of the sort described in this book were typically not the norm. Deliberately partnering with groups of schools has been a hallmark of the LSM to increase this type of sharing in order to capitalise on the capability that exists across schools and to better meet the challenge of scaling effectiveness. We have had to build such capability for across-school collaboration very directly through the PLCs. But other countries and/or jurisdictions may already have norms, values and practices as well as better structures for across-school collaborations, and may need less focus in building capability in these areas.

Interestingly, in NZ, structures are currently being redesigned to change the autonomy, and move to greater collaboration across schools nationally. In part this reflects how the LSM has both been influenced by and has contributed to policy shifts in NZ, in particular towards a new role in and across schools leading evidence-based collaboration (McNaughton, 2017).

The significance of partnerships in NZ extends to the position of the indigenous community in the wider education system. The founding NZ document, The Treaty of Waitangi, was signed between indigenous Māori and the Crown. This document affords indigenous Māori a dual set of rights as tangata whenua (original inhabitants on NZ), and affords Māori culture a special place within NZ in general (a multicultural society underpinned by bicultural foundations) and educationally (e.g. in the NZ Curriculum [Ministry of Education, 2007]). This positioning thus necessitates partnerships and is reflected in the partnership approach of the LSM.

We maintain that developing partnerships that are capable of co-design, where there is mutual respect and agency can be used in countries with a different view of school relationships with their communities including with researchers. In different countries, we have strived to develop such agency and power with the local schools and teachers, for example, through the collaborative analysis process which allows schools and teachers' knowledge to be tested equally alongside researcher knowledge and which puts teachers and school leaders in the position of co-designers of resources.

A third related feature is how teachers are positioned to be innovative problem solvers. There is long celebrated history of teachers as innovators inventing tools and practices in the NZ context. One example is the natural language texts for learning to read which were invented by NZ teachers early in the twentieth century who were teaching in what was then called the Native schools (rural Māori schools) (McNaughton, 2001). This innovation was in response to the imported English texts about snow, robins and larks, and Janet and John, which did not work well in the local context. Another well-known example is the NZ designed early intervention called Reading Recovery (McNaughton, 2014). Thirdly, the NZ curriculum view of teachers is as inquirers who are capable of being 'adaptive experts' (Ministry of Education, 2007). Finally, the curriculum itself, both in the English and Maori versions, is light on prescriptions. Teachers are expected to take what is a framework with some guiding descriptions of progressions and enact it through their own design as a local curriculum. Coupled with the autonomy of schools this is both an enabler and a constraint. The constraint is that this puts a lot of pressure on the capability of the individual teacher to be able to design for the local context.

Finally, the NZ Education system adopts a plurality of data and research methodologies – eschewing a single data source or assessment as evidence. Even the National Standards which were required to be reported every year for accountability to their communities were based on overall teacher judgments and teachers were explicitly told to rely on a range of data including their own observations to judge students against a standard (Ministry of Education, n.d.-b). With a recent change in government these standards have been removed from mandatory requirements, so there is even more emphasis on forming expert judgments from a variety of sources for feedback to parents and to judge effectiveness. This emphasis of judgment is supported by and reflected in key national Ministry documents, such as the Ministry's Best Evidence Synthesis series where a range of research methodologies, not just RCTs, are accepted as robust evidence (e.g. Timperley et al., 2007). This broader view of student learning as including but not limited to student achievement is perhaps best seen in the valued learning outcomes for indigenous students (Māori) which include having Māori identity, language and culture valued (Ministry of Education, n.d.-c). This approach to assessment, for example, allows for an emphasis on collaborative analysis of achievement data and a relentless focus on achievement using a range of assessments without the 'baggage' of high stakes assessment.

Teachers are thus more likely to openly discuss strengths and weaknesses in teaching and learning. Similarly principals are more likely to be open about a school's strengths and weaknesses and take calculated risks to improve teaching and learning as their funding is not dependent on their academic results and they can make these decisions with their local communities who they are accountable to. But the potential risk is that teachers need detailed understanding of the strengths and weaknesses of the data sources and the role of standardised and informal assessments without which the validity and reliability of the judgments can be compromised. This underlines the importance of cross checking built into the uses of data in the LSM.

Chapter Three

Collaborative Data Analysis

Collaborative analysis of data is one of two key concepts that underpin the LSM and serves multiple functions. It is used for intervention design and redesign; it is an important form of resourcing and PLD for school partners; it is the means to develop and strengthen partnerships; and it is used to sustain the intervention when the partnerships reach a natural conclusion. Collaborative analysis is not just central to many LSM activities; it is the glue which integrates all components of the LSM.

We unpack the complexity of this process across several chapters but start here with a description of what the standard analysis requires of participants. We have left the word 'collaborative' in the chapter, as all the analyses are undertaken in collaboration and to retain the emphasis on its collaborative nature. In later chapters, we describe collaborative analysis of data in relation to partnerships (Chapter Four), resourcing and PLD (Chapter Five), sustainability (Chapter Six) and researchers learning through cycles of design and evaluation (Chapter Seven).

Much has been written about the typical data analysis process in educational settings (e.g. Schildkamp et al., 2018), and it is not our intention to revisit this material. Moreover, rather than write about the steps in the analysis process as a series of discrete and formulaic steps, here we wish to underscore the iterative and dynamic nature of the process and the conditions needed to change teaching practices. So we start by briefly describing the analysis process, then discuss how to make principled decisions about the kinds of student and practice data to collect including a discussion on what counts as quality data. This chapter focusses on student learning and teaching and school practice data, although other kinds of data are briefly mentioned. An extended example is provided which explains and then illustrates the analysis process from Phase 1: Profiling where the purpose is to contextualise effective practice to local contexts using data about student and teaching strengths and learning needs. We end the chapter with a discussion of the artefacts for data analysis, which serve multiple purposes in the LSM, and a caveat on this process.

Research-practice Partnerships for School Improvement:
The Learning Schools Model, 37–56
Copyright © 2020 by Mei Kuin Lai, Stuart McNaughton, Rebecca Jesson and Aaron Wilson
Published under exclusive license
doi:10.1108/978-1-78973-571-020201004

The Analysis Process

Our definition of data, as defined and discussed in previous chapters, allows for the multiple kinds that teachers and school leaders need for decision-making. It is deliberately broad to include any relevant information about students, parents, schools and teachers derived from both qualitative and quantitative methods of analysis (Lai & Schildkamp, 2013). In the LSM, as discussed in Chapter Two, the analysis of data is aligned theoretically to data use for evidence-based teacher inquiry, as opposed to data use for accountability. That is, data are used to support teachers and/or school leaders to understand and manage their own data, identify strengths and weaknesses and root causes for the weaknesses and then determine an appropriate solution to address those weaknesses and capitalise on the strengths.

The process for analysing data is similar in function to other analysis models (e.g. Earl & Katz, 2006; Marsh, 2012). A purpose or goal is established for data analysis, hypotheses for data collection that inform the purpose are generated; relevant data to test these hypotheses are collected, analysed and interpreted; actions are taken based on the analysis and interpretation; and these actions are evaluated against the original hypotheses and used to inform practice. The cycle is iterative in that the interpretation of data often leads to further data being selected and collected, and/or analysed. The process is also iterative in that the evaluation of the action taken results in a further cycle of data analysis to address new findings from the data analysis process and refine the actions to be taken. Fig. 2 adapted from Lai and Schildkamp (2013) shows this process:

There are four key emphases in the LSM data analysis process that differentiate it from more generic data analysis processes (Lai & McNaughton, 2016):

1. a focus on collecting both data on valued student outcomes and data on teaching and school practices with an emphasis on data on teaching practices;
2. the development of a co-designed solution from the analysis process as opposed to 'buying' an off-the-shelf intervention that could address the problem;
3. the use of agreed evaluation criteria to test the adequacy of multiple hypotheses and solutions developed from the analyses process; and
4. a focus on PCK to develop hypotheses and co-design solutions.

1. A Focus on Both Valued Student Outcomes and Practices

In Chapter Two, we laid out the argument that much of the process and content generated through the LSM needs to be contextualised. Each of the design features of the LSM – the process of gathering evidence, the development of reasonable hypotheses about possible solutions and the solutions themselves – are developed and located within the local context. The local context is viewed through an ecological systems lens, where student learning is best understood in relation to the interactions between the child and others within the immediate

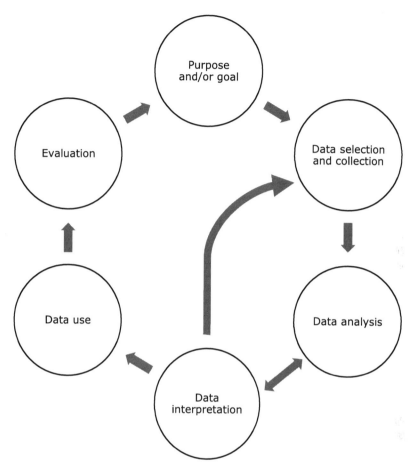

Fig. 2.   Typical Data Analysis Process.

context (classroom) and the wider contexts in which that child is located (school and beyond). Contextualisation thus requires the collection, analysis and understanding of local evidence. This means collecting data on students, the classroom and the school and in some cases, beyond (such as family practices and neighbourhood resources).

Data on valued student outcomes are agreed by all partners in the LSM, and these are typically outcomes of student learning (the focus of this chapter). Importantly, valued student outcomes and student learning are not synonymous with student achievement data. They may (and have been in some of our studies) focussed on non-academic areas of learning including social and emotional skills. But if there is an achievement focus, appropriate and agreed assessments, standardised or not, and triangulated with each other and with other data can provide relevant and useful data to determine acceleration in learning.

In the case of student learning, relevant data on teaching and school practices to be collected are determined by the patterns in student learning that are revealed in the analyses of the student data. Thus the process of analysing student data results in a profile of their strengths and learning needs, and the data on teaching and school practices are collected to best understand the relationships between the student profile and the contexts in which that learning takes place. Given the ecological systems lens what data may be potentially relevant can only be fully determined *after* the collection of the data on student learning. Typically, the sequence is collecting data on student learning followed by data on teaching and school practices, and sometimes other data where appropriate (e.g. family practices).

In the LSM, we foreground teaching over school practices. This is firstly because, as per our ecological systems framing, teachers are the students' immediate context for learning, and as such, teachers have a direct influence on student learning unlike school leaders, whose influence is often mediated by teachers. Secondly, we view changing teaching practices as catalytic, in that changes in teaching are highly likely to improve student learning outcomes. Research that informed our initial thinking about the model indicated that the quality of teaching contributes a large proportion of the variance in outcomes for students (Hattie, 2009), and thus it would be beneficial to place our emphasis in this space. The focus on teaching practice has also been refined, with findings over time and across LSM projects in different contexts which suggests that our initial emphasis on improving teaching practices has improved achievement (e.g. see Jesson, McNaughton, Wilson et al., 2018; Lai & McNaughton, 2016).

2. Co-designed Solutions from the Analysis

Data analysis looks different in different interventions, and interventions often take difference stances on whether the analysis results in a solution that is researcher-designed, practitioner-designed or co-designed. For example, the Centre for Data-Driven Reform in Education states that a key purpose in data analysis is to select an intervention from a series of interventions that have met their suggested criteria for having demonstrated success (Centre for Data-Driven Reform, 2011).

Our focus is on a co-designed solution (or solutions) created by researchers and school leaders/teachers to address the issues identified through the data analysis process. The solution is not prescribed by researchers; nor is it left to school leaders and teachers to determine the solution for themselves. Rather, a range of likely solutions is discussed by researchers, school leaders and teachers, and jointly selected to be tested. The partner who is primarily responsible for developing the co-designed solution varies according to the context of the project and the nature of the problem to be solved. In some applications, the researchers' role in developing the co-designed solution was foregrounded, for example, where they adapted or designed effective practices for PLD, and where school leaders designed ways of implementing these practices that were coherent and effective in their own settings. In other applications, the school leaders' role was foregrounded, in that the design of the solution was initially developed by them to address an identified need, and the researchers used the collaborative analysis process to inform that design.

3. Agreed Criteria for Evaluating Hypotheses

If solutions are co-designed, then there needs to be a process for testing hypotheses and their related solutions. Evaluation criteria are adopted for this purpose to adjudicate between competing hypotheses and solutions. Having agreed evaluation criteria is particularly important in the LSM, because there are potentially multiple hypotheses from teachers, school leaders and researchers' about the problem to be collectively solved, and multiple solutions to address the problem based on the various hypotheses. Without agreed evaluation criteria to judge the validity of the hypotheses and solutions, there may be tendency to privilege researcher or practitioner hypotheses and solutions (Robinson & Lai, 2006). At best, this means agreement on a series of possible solutions which if implemented do no harm but add no value; at worst, inaccurate or ineffective practices that are detrimental to practice and student outcomes are agreed on. Agreed evaluation criteria is also particularly useful in mitigating against confirmation bias, that is the tendency to search for, interpret, favour and recall information in a way that confirms one's pre-existing beliefs or hypotheses.

A specific evaluative framework that has informed our thinking on shared evaluation criteria is problem-based methodology (Robinson & Lai, 2006). They proposed four standards to evaluate theories-of-action: accuracy (empirical claims about practice are well founded in evidence); effectiveness (theories meet the goals and values of those who hold them); coherence (competing theories from outside perspectives are considered, and solutions introduced in one setting do not create problems in another); and improvability (theories and solutions can be adapted to meet changing needs or incorporate new goals, values and contextual constraints). The four standards go beyond searching for evidence for hypotheses or proposed solutions as the only way of evaluating its adequacy, in that a 'good' hypothesis or 'good solution' must have more than just evidence supporting it. For example, it is possible to create a good evidence-based solution for literacy that is so time intensive there is little time for mathematics instruction, thereby solving the literacy problem but creating one in mathematics (i.e. the solution has failed the standard of coherence). The four standards are not used in a formulaic way or as a set of prescriptive steps, but they inform our thinking when we examine and discuss the data. For example, when discussing data, our focus is on evidence for claims (standard of accuracy), and data are examined in light of the purposes and goals of the partnership (standard of effectiveness). There is an emphasis on both research and practitioner hypotheses and solutions with an emphasis on ensuring solutions do not violate what is known to be effective practice (standard of coherence); and there is a strong focus on continuous cycles of data analysis and inquiry (standard of improvability). We have also learned that possible solutions need to be judged in terms of how well they can meet the systemic challenges of capability building, sustainability, scalability, variability and acceleration discussed in the first chapter. Again, such criteria are not used formulaically but they inform our thinking during the analysis process.

4. Pedagogical Content Knowledge

A final emphasis is on the knowledge required to effectively analyse and use data. Such knowledge is not just knowledge about how to analyse and use data (e.g. how to carry out the steps in the analysis process). It is also the PCK (Shulman, 1986), that is the knowledge of the content-area and how to teach it, required to effectively analyse and use data pertaining to a particular content-area. For example, a decade ago, we argued that effective analysis and use of data in reading comprehension requires knowledge about comprehension acquisition and effective pedagogy in teaching reading comprehension, and we demonstrated through our work that such knowledge is required to develop and test hypotheses to improve achievement in reading comprehension (Lai & McNaughton, 2009). This focus has been an emphasis since the start of our work, and is consistent with newer conceptions of the analysis process and data literacy that include PCK as critical to conceptual frameworks of data literacy (Gummer & Mandinach, 2015). Thus, analysis of data cannot be separated from the content-area that is the focus of the analysis, and PCK in that content-area is required in terms of all the steps of the analysis process. It is required to develop and frame meaningful hypotheses, to determine appropriate assessments that can address the hypotheses, to analyse and then interpret the emerging data and to co-design practices based on the analysis of data.

Principles for Data Collection

The emphasis in the LSM on collecting data on both student learning and teaching and school practices can feel overwhelming for partners. So how do researchers, school leaders and teachers collaboratively decide on what data to collect? The principles for collecting and analysing student learning data (typically in the form of achievement data from assessments) and school and teaching data are identical to those outlined in the standard analysis process (Fig. 2).

Data Fit for Purpose

Firstly, the data collected needs to be fit for purpose, in that only data that meet the purposes and aims of the partnerships are collected. For example, if the purpose is to improve achievement in writing, then achievement data on writing should be collected and analysed, followed by a collection of data on teaching and school practices that supports the understanding of, or can explain, the achievement data in writing. In the case of writing, this can include an examination of reading data in relation to writing to understand whether the issue is solely with productive use of language (writing), or a more generalised problem with written language where the students struggle with both productive and receptive (reading) knowledge and skills. While a focus on collecting data fit for purpose may seem prosaic, in our experience over 15 years and in line with what others have found, we have encountered numerous instances where data that are available are what is collected, rather than what is actually required for the purpose; or where data are collected without a clear purpose (e.g. Schildkamp & Kuiper, 2010).

There are features of the measures or assessments that are necessary to achieve the multiple purposes for collaborative data analysis. Features include repeatability and multifunctionality. Often, and especially in the case of achievement data, there is a need for repeated assessments. The same standardised assessments are used to develop context specific profiles, to provide feedback to partners on progress towards achieving valued outcomes and to measure the impact on achievement after each phase and at the end of each project. Other sources of data may be one off to help test the adequacy of initial hypotheses. In NZ, there are appropriate repeatable assessments that we use that provide both information on progress over time and information on student strengths and weaknesses required for developing such profiles. Where such assessments are not available, we work with local partners to develop them.

The purpose for data collection can either be strongly shared by all partners at the start (e.g. an agreement to improve reading comprehension) or the process of analysing the data can be used to develop a shared purpose (e.g. demonstrating that there is a need to focus on achievement data). By this we mean, that sometimes partners have a more developed understanding of the urgent problem to be addressed, and data collection is used to check their understanding and to deepen it. In other situations, the data collection is more exploratory as the extent and nature of the problem is less well understood (See Chapter Two case studies for two different starting points for data collection, and how that impacted on the breadth and intensity of data collection).

The problem or issue the partnership is trying to solve, which in its generic form is often one of how to be more effective, can be ill-structured or well structured (Robinson, 1993). Ill-structured problems are problems when there are no obvious criteria for how to solve the problem, no definable procedures for reaching a solution and uncertainty about the information required to solve the problem. Most educational problems, like most meaningful real-world problems, are of the ill-structured variety (Frederiksen, 1984). For example, solving an ill-structured problem of linking teaching practices to student achievement is an iterative process of repeated cycles of developing, testing and revising hypotheses about what combinations of instructional events best address students' learning needs. This requires openness in rethinking and revising initial hypotheses of teaching practices, where ambiguity is tolerated and judgment reserved until there is more evidence to gain clarity about the hypotheses (Earl & Timperley, 2008). It does not matter whether there is agreement on the purpose prior to data collection, as cycles of data analysis can be used to become increasingly more specific about the purpose and related hypotheses, to develop measures to turn ill-structured problems into well-structured ones and to develop a shared understanding around the purpose.

When there are multiple purposes or competing hypotheses of ill-structured problems, there are multiple possible criteria for how to solve the problem, less definable procedures for reaching a solution, and uncertainty about the information required to solve the problem. This presents a pragmatic problem. It may not be financially possible, practical or appropriate to test all possible hypotheses. We have solved this conundrum in several ways. Given that the LSM is typically a partnership between schools and researchers, we firstly only focus on purposes and hypotheses that are within the school and researcher's core business and within their control. For example, in one application there was a large problem with students who were transient, that is, those who entered or left within an academic year. This issue has been linked to wider issues of adequate housing (Gilbert, 2005), but even if the hypothesis of housing was proven by the data, it is not the school's core business to solve housing issues, nor is it something within their control. As such, this hypothesis was not tested.

A second approach is to eliminate hypotheses raised in discussions where the logic of the argument is weaker than other hypotheses. For example, in another application, the argument was that it was changes in hormones that resulted in the low achievement for that particular group of schools. However, change in hormones would be applicable to all students of similar age nationally, and the logic of the argument that hormones resulted in lower achievement for a particular cluster of schools was weaker than for other hypotheses, and therefore not tested. It is possible, however to have multiple compelling hypotheses to test. In which case, we focus on what we call 'catalytic' variables, which is a focus on only testing what is hypothesised based on previous research and experience to be most likely to impact on valued outcomes and meet the five big systemic challenges.

High-Quality Data

As well as being relevant to the purpose, data has to be of high quality. Such 'quality data' are robust and trustworthy. In terms of the achievement data collected through assessments, we would require that such data be valid and reliable, and where possible, psychometric robustness. By valid, we mean both content validity that is data that can actually measure to a strong degree the content we wish to measure, and face validity, in that it is accepted by schools as appropriate to measure student learning in their context. Assessment data also need to meet acceptable standards of reliability, for example, that repeated measures of the assessment used to gather data will yield similar results. In order to meet these criteria for valid and reliable data, where possible, we use nationally approved standardised tests that report on reliability and validity, and where there is face validity. However, we still discuss the assessments that we use with schools so that there is an agreement that these are the best assessments to use. Where such assessments do not exist, researchers work with partners to develop purpose built assessments and use principles underpinning content and face validity and reliability to test the appropriateness and robustness of the purpose built assessment measures. In this way, we adhere as closely as possible to what is considered reliable and valid in the research literature on assessments.

Similarly, we require the data on teaching and school practices (and beyond) to be robust and trustworthy. Given our sequence of collecting only teaching and school (and beyond) data that can support the understanding of patterns in student learning, the kinds of data on practices collected and how they are then analysed varies across LSM applications. However, we would expect each type of data and their associated analysis to adhere to the standards of high-quality data appropriate for that type of data and analysis. For example, if we collect data to check whether certain features of instruction (e.g. feedback) are absent or present in a lesson, we would expect that the standard methodological rigour for these forms of observations be applied. This include: an operational definition of feedback that is defined in a way that repeated observations by the same observer or across observers would yield similar data; and a defined sampling method for observations such as interval sampling that can be reliably use across observations and observers.

Principles for Data Analysis and Use: An Extended Example

Full rationales for every aspect of analysis used in the LSM are in the respective articles about the LSM referenced in Chapters One and Two. While the analyses used to test hypotheses depend on the nature of the data they always adhere to the typical standards of rigour for that type of analysis. For example, if it is possible to use statistical analyses, the analyses must be appropriate, meet the standards for robust statistical analysis, and be as high an order of statistical analyses as possible. Moreover, because there is a tendency to view quantitative forms of analysis uncritically (Fjørtoft & Lai, 2019), any statistical analyses, particularly statistical modelling, that we conduct is strongly grounded in the study's purpose and an appropriate theoretical framework that drives the kind of analyses we undertake. We are also cognisant and explicit about the statistical decisions that could influence different statistical models and how that in turn influences the results.

The use of statistical procedures in partnerships carries with it a communicative imperative. It is to translate the procedures and results in ways that are meaningful to the partnership and the meaning making needed to judge outcomes and to design and redesign to meet the shared objectives. When significance tests and effect sizes are used, we translate these into realistic estimates of educational significance. Acceleration for example might be judged as having happened if the effect size is moderate such as ES=0.20. But what that means in terms of a years expected growth might be the most useful metric. In writing for example, the use of the standardised assessments will be discussed in terms of statistical significance but also how many weeks of extra growth, or how many weeks below or above nationally expected levels a cohort is. By the end of an application cycle we would have often developed with partners a high level summary of the outcomes which provides real-world metrics.

Similarly, if qualitative thematic analyses are used, we require such analyses to meet the standard of rigour for thematic analyses, with similar notions of ensuring the rationale for decision-making around particular analyses are clear and defendable. The same applies for case studies, which we have used as a means for understanding variability and to identify what is currently working well and might be part of the solution. We adhere to best practice for case studies.

Much has been written about the steps for analysis, and our intention as outlined at the start of this chapter is to present an account of collaborative analysis of data in way that captures the iterative and dynamic nature of the process. Thus, here, we describe an extended case study of the analysis process from Phase 1: Profiling to illustrate the typical analyses in an LSM application where the focus is to contextualise effective practice to local contexts using the collaborative analysis process. This example serves to illustrate the iterative and dynamic process of analysing data that is similar to the collaborative analysis processes used across all LSM phases, and thus is a useful example of how to analyse, interpret and use data more generally.

This example is from the Phase 1: Profiling in two of our applications ($n=13$ schools) (Lai & McNaughton, 2009). The applications were interventions to improve student achievement in reading comprehension, and this was a shared purpose. However, at the start of the project, the full extent of the achievement issues and the context-specific student and teacher strengths and weaknesses relating to these issues were unknown. The extended example illustrates how we analysed and used data to develop a context-specific profile of strengths and weaknesses in reading comprehension, and matched those to context-specific teaching strengths and needs. We then analysed profiles in relation to effective practices in the literature to co-design resources that built on strengths and addresses weaknesses. This example extends the case study of the more tightly defined problem in Chapter Two, and complements the second case study in Chapter Two, where the problem was less defined or agreed on, and where there were greater disagreements and/or uncertainty about the nature of the problem.

Typical Analyses: Achievement

There is a set of standard analyses used when the purpose is to develop context-specific profiles of student strengths' and weaknesses in a content-area, and this is similar across all LSM projects. Given this purpose, the set of analyses aim to (a) Determine the *extent* of the achievement problem using agreed comparisons for determining whether there is a problem and the extent of the problem and (b) determine the *nature* of the problem through a detailed content-area focussed diagnosis of students' strengths and learning needs in the content-area under investigation.

It is important to have an agreed point of comparison to determine the extent of the problem, as different points of comparison can result in different conclusions about the extent of the problem, and decisions about which comparison to use are value laden. For example, it is possible for a group of students to score better than students in similar lower socio-economic communities, but score much worse than students nationally. So, if the comparison is students in similar schools, then one could conclude that these students do not have an achievement problem. Comparisons can include norms, that is, how the students perform relative to a group used for norming. This can be, for example, a national norm from a nationally representative sample or the norm for a particular group, such as the norm for schools in similar socio-economic communities. A comparison could be a target, which may be a national policy target such as 85% of school leavers to have attained the secondary school leaving certificate, and the development of such targets can be aspirational and/or based on existing data that are analysed to determine challenging but achievable targets for a community. Comparisons can also be made against the appropriate curriculum level which may be higher or lower than the norms, in that the national curriculum levels for a particular age group are higher than the curriculum levels scored by the norming sample. In our work, we use multiple comparisons which are both local (i.e. how the groups of schools in the LSM are performing) as well as national, in terms of national norms and curriculum level expectations. We always include national points of comparison in our work because of the value that we and the schools we work with place on students being able to perform as well as other students nationally. As a community member once told one of us (paraphrased here):

> Only comparing our school to other schools in lower socio-economic groups sends us the message that you have low expectations of our students and our community. Our students need to be able to compete on a global scale, and can perform as well as other students nationally.

To measure how students perform compared to an agreed point of comparison, multiple analyses are conducted: (a) average achievement against the point of comparison as measured by appropriate measures of central tendency (e.g. mean and medians), (b) distribution of achievement that is the spread of scores and (c) variability by subgroup such as by age, ethnicity or classroom. Ethnicity is of particular importance in the context of the work we do, as our work has focussed on reducing the gap between indigenous and ethnic minority students from Pacific nations, and other students. Starting achievement levels are important for examining data over time as our work has consistently shown variations in achievement gain from different starting levels (e.g. Lai et al., 2011). Given our commitment to building on strengths and capitalising on variability, we focus on examining variability to uncover pockets of promising practice or to develop case studies of effective teachers. The spread of scores in a distribution and variability across subgroups also provide important information for the intervention design. For example, a wide spread of reading achievement in a class requires teachers be skilled in teaching multiple reading levels, typically through grouping, which in turn requires skills in behaviour management of groups. It could also be that the low achievement is not uniform across the school, but within a particular subgroup, and that the intervention needs to be targeted at that group.

Example

Data were collected from the schools using two standardised tests in reading comprehension. Data were analysed firstly against the national norms to examine what the local student achievement patterns looked like in relation to national expectations in the form of national norms. Two main comparisons were made. Firstly the average stanine scores were compared to the national average (i.e. the mean stanine score was compared to the expected average of stanine 5 [stanines are a method of scaling test scores on a nine-point standard scale with a mean of five (5) and a standard deviation of two (2) with 9 being the highest stanine], Elley, 2001). Secondly, the distribution of achievement was compared to the national distribution, for example, bar graphs of students in each stanine band compared to the nationally expected percentage in each stanine band. The latter was important because the goal was not just for particular groups that have been underachieving to come to function at average bands. Rather, in the ideal case, the distribution of students needed to approximate an expected distribution – in the case of NZ students, the NZ national distribution. The analyses further examined subgroups of students below, at or above expected national norms or curriculum levels (e.g. by gender and age), identified the amount of variance from the national expectations and identified any patterns in the data, for example, large numbers below expectations, outliers or scores that were much higher or lower than the rest, and wide/small spread. These analyses showed that on average students were about two years below national expectations in both subtests, the distribution of achievement was skewed to the left with more students in the lower stanine bands, and that was little subgroup variation.

Knowing students' overall scores relative to an agreed comparison point is important, but it does not contain the detail required to use the information formatively. That is, we also need an analysis of the specific student strengths and learning issues that contributed to the overall scores. The next step is to carry out a detailed diagnosis on the information in the assessments to uncover students' strengths and learning needs, typically using existing diagnostic information contained in the assessments. Some assessments include subtests that can be analysed statistically; some also contain open-ended questions that can be analysed thematically.

Example

We closely examined students' strengths and weaknesses in their assessments to understand why students scored two years below national expectations. One test, the STAR (Elley, 2001) comprised of subtests where each subtest focussed on an important area of reading comprehension such as paragraph comprehension and vocabulary. Analysis was of subtest scores and qualitatively coding the types of errors students made on one of the subtests according to the types of errors reported in the STAR manual (Elley, 2001). The subtest scores showed that students in general had a strength in decoding and sentence comprehension, and weaknesses in vocabulary and paragraph comprehension as assessed by a cloze passage test. A subtest analysis of the vocabulary subtest showed that the majority of students (70%) scored below the national expectation and of that 70%, 40% scored below what the test manual considered a 'critical score'. Paragraph comprehension scores were similarly low. An examination of the errors in one subtest (cloze passage) showed that students used words which were close but not accurate (e.g. giraffe eats branches, rather than leaves), and that idiomatic or figurative uses were problematic (e.g. students substituted 'pretty' face or 'ugly' face for the required 'rock' face). In the second standardised test, students read different passages of different genres (e.g. myth, informational text) and answered a mix of inference and factual questions. An analysis was conducted to check whether students performed equally well on these different types of questions and across different kinds of comprehension passages. Students, for example, performed equally poorly on inferential and factual items, and preformed less well when the comprehension passages were more complex such as reading and answering questions about a myth (Lai, McNaughton, MacDonald, & Farry, 2004).

Typical Analyses: Teaching and School Data

While the context-specific profiles of learning indicate areas of strengths and weaknesses, there are numerous possible hypotheses relating to teaching and school practices that could explain these profiles. Rather than assume what the causes are from experience or the literature, we test the proposed causes (framed as hypotheses) by collecting data about these causes and examining the relationship between the causes and the profiles of student learning. This typically involves identifying the possible causes from the literature, from collaborative discussion with partners and from previous data; developing measures to collect data on the causes; and then analysing that data. We start by analysing the data on teaching and school practices separately, and then analyse them in relationship with achievement patterns. This often requires iterative cycles of inquiry that become increasingly more specified about the causes and their relationship with achievement. We also pay close attention to variability, such as variability across classrooms to understand the causes, uncover effective practices in situ and to determine the range of practices for future interventions. This deliberate process of hypothesis testing reduces confirmation bias, as it deliberately forces researchers and school partners to consider the evidence for multiple hypotheses rather than foreclose on preferred hypotheses and only seek evidence for those. It also guards against the tendency to jump from the data to an action without understanding or testing the reasons for the patterns in the data.

Example

Classroom observations using in situ running records of events were carried out by the second author early in the first year of the intervention to understand the current teaching with the aim of matching patterns of teaching with achievement patterns that is the process of examining the relationship between the patterns in achievement with the patterns in teaching. Classrooms were nominated by each of the schools and selected to represent age levels within schools. Instruction in these classrooms was observed for 40–60 minutes during the usual scheduled session within which the teaching and learning of reading comprehension occurred. The observer recorded large and small group activities. Details of types of texts and other general features were noted based on the existing knowledge-base of effective teaching in reading comprehension. Interactions were recorded as close to verbatim as possible, recognising that capturing dialogue on the run meant that the record was incomplete. Notes and commentary were made alongside the running records.

The analytic frame for observing drew from the research literature on reading comprehension and teaching, and emerging evidence from assessments collected from the local context. The observer therefore paid special attention to discourse structures, topics and tasks known to relate to aspects of reading comprehension such as comprehension strategies, decoding, content knowledge and vocabulary. Features of teaching were attended to such as the forms and functions taken by instances of practice and deliberate acts of teaching such as feedback, modelling and prompting. Variations between teachers and within a teachers' lesson were also noted. The running records with notes and commentaries provided an accumulating base for emerging hypotheses. The observer, who was the second author in this book and a Professor in Literacy, was knowledgeable of the research and theory relating to instruction in general and reading comprehension in particular, as well as the features of the achievement data.

Typical Analyses: The Relationship between Teaching and School Data and Achievement Data

The process of mapping evidence from school and teaching data to achievement data has several stages typical of the process for solving ill-structured problems (Robinson, 1993). The first stage involved examining the achievement data to determine the profiles of student learning, then developing hypotheses about the teaching and school practices that might be associated with achievement, and collecting data on those. The hypotheses of the links between teaching and school practices, and profiles of student learning are then firmed up recursively, in this extended example, firmed up as the observational process was repeated across classrooms and subsequently across applications of the LSM. This firming up process requires testing the emerging hypotheses against new data collected across classrooms, including examining the new data for disconfirming hypotheses (Robinson, 1993). This also resulted in new hypotheses and new understandings of the inter-relationships between existing hypotheses.

The observations produced several hypotheses which were tested and refined over the next four years across two applications of the model. Because each hypothesis required different domain knowledge, we limited our illustration to one domain, that of vocabulary learning in the next section, where we discuss putting the two sources of data (teaching and achievement) together.

Example

The achievement data showed that vocabulary scores were low, indeed lower than national norms and the second lowest of the subtest scores across years and levels. Several features of the achievement data were also hypothesised to be influenced by the low vocabulary scores. For example, we had been surprised to find, contrary to predictions, that both factual and inferential items tended to be similarly low, suggesting that a major stumbling block was some general feature of vocabulary and sentence comprehension restricting the identification of which text units to recall, or to use to infer. We knew that in general decoding, accuracy and speed did not appear to be impediments given high scores in the decoding subtest a test corroborated by data collected by the schools themselves (Lai et al., 2004). In addition, error patterns on the Cloze subtest of the STAR suggested a general approach which looked like guessing. Words that were fitted to the sentence made sense in the pre gap context but not in the post gap context. The errors also revealed that idiomatic or figurative uses might be problematic. Teachers' comments confirmed that vocabulary was an issue for students, and informal conversations with children also added to the picture of difficulties.

There were multiple possible hypotheses for the vocabulary issues identified in the data. The beginning hypothesis based on the literature was that the vocabulary instruction was somehow insufficient. So one of the focusses of the first set of observations following the achievement analysis was on examples of explicit vocabulary instruction and repetitions and practice. Thus in the running records of the classrooms, the observer noted possible new vocabulary introduced in tasks and instances where explicit vocabulary instruction took place. Notes of instances of good practice and queries were jotted on the sheets. Examples include: '[many instances of] technical terms. .questioning sometimes guess'; and, 'still few instances of going back to the text to check'.

Further discussion with colleagues and examining the research literature added to the fine-grained hypotheses by providing sources of knowledge for reflection and peer critique. A summary of the hypotheses in development was prepared and fed back and discussed with the senior group of school leaders. The feedback also utilised artefacts in the form of transcripts and examples from running records together with detailed commentary. The section relating to vocabulary made the following points. Estimates from the field notes suggested quite a high frequency of explicit instruction of vocabulary; six to seven instances occurred on average across the classrooms where the meaning of vocabulary (including technical terms) was specifically identified or elaborated on. Many of the instances of vocabulary interactions involved referring to and defining technical terms. Terms were used for linguistic categories at sub word (e.g. blend), word (e.g. noun), sentence (e.g. passive voice), text structure (e.g. paragraph) and text types (e.g. narrative), and the exchanges were often associated with the teaching of strategies and the use of technical terms such as 'clarifying', 'predicting' and 'visualising'.

These aforementioned findings and other aspects of the verbatim records suggested two issues. Firstly, this suggested that the situation was not as simple as insufficient interaction overall, rather the rate of these interactions occurring for any individual child may have been lower than what was needed. This hypothesis is suggested by a classroom record in which 25 teacher–student interactions occurred in the course of a 20-minute session. Whilst generally frequent, this resulted in an average of one interaction per student. The focus on any one particular word occurred once and there was little evidence of repeated opportunities to use or elaborate that word. The second issue, made more obvious in the analyses of strategy teaching, was that meanings were seldom checked in ways that elaborated specific connotations in context. Many of the instances involved discussion of students' ideas about meanings but often the teacher accepted student contributions without critical appraisal. Few of the instances involved explicit instruction and modelling of how to check meanings within texts or via a dictionary or a thesaurus. This pattern was judged to undermine accurately learning the sematic complexity of specific words as well as building the form of metalinguistic awareness called word consciousness.

The teachers discussed with the researchers the specific hypothesis that there was a need to increase the rate of vocabulary acquisition across students in ways that gave access to multiple meanings and connotations in context. Research evidence to support the need to boost vocabulary through teacher guidance in elaborations and feedback was identified during this process (e.g. Biemiller, 1999). Some general ways that were discussed included the increased use of reading to small groups with carefully selected texts which provided variation in genre and topic, and planned rates of exposure to new vocabulary. In addition, language acquisition research which noted how increased extended talk was associated with new vocabulary and with greater understanding of complex utterances was introduced (e.g. Hart & Risley, 1995).

This hypothesis was used as a basis for planning resourcing and PLD sessions with teachers in Phase 2. In that year more systematic observations using in situ observations and video recording were made and based on this emerging hypothesis. More quantitative analyses (using the basic unit of instructional exchange) were based on video records as well as case studies of whole lessons of teachers. At the beginning of the second phase, 15 classrooms including at least two from each school were observed, again classrooms were nominated and selected to represent age levels.

In sum, analyses to contextualise effective practice to local context-specific profiles of teaching and learning are an iterative and on-going process. Such analyses are not just conducted across multiple years within an LSM application, but stretch across multiple applications. This results in a body of knowledge built over time both within an application and across applications. For example, the hypotheses discussed here became even more fine-grained throughout the second year of the same group of schools, as material was discussed in the PLD sessions and as more systematic observations were added to the evidence base together with case study data. The same process was repeated in another application with a second neighbouring cluster of schools. In this cluster there was a virtually identical issue with vocabulary primarily identified through the profiling of achievement. Information from this cluster added considerably to the specificity of the hypothesis. For example, while similar patterns of teaching were found, there were new ones that were somewhat different from the first cluster. Analysis of classroom observations in the second cluster of schools therefore confirmed the general hypothesis about vocabulary instruction from the first cluster, but uncovered a new hypothesis in this context that was not present in the previous context, namely that there were high rates of teacher questions, often in the form of Initiate–Respond–Evaluate (IRE) sequences (Cazden, 2001). Questions were present in over a third of the exchanges, they were almost double those in which the teacher commented on the meanings of words, and considerably higher than exchanges which looked at meanings in dictionaries. A high rate of teacher questioning can reduce the complexity of children's learning by dampening children's contributions (Wood, 1998), and the focus was getting the right balance for a particular classroom.

Artefacts for Collaborative Analysis

Artefacts are programmes, policies and procedures that are designed and used to influence practice, and can include for example daily schedules, meetings and agendas (Halverson, 2003). Artefacts form a large part of how the collaborative analysis is enacted in our model, and these artefacts have been refined over time through subsequent LSM iterations based on our own reflections of their efficacy and school leader and teacher feedback.

In every application of the LSM, there are two primary artefacts. The first is reports, PowerPoints and slide show presentations which summarise and interpret the analyses of student learning, which is the typical valued student outcome in our work. When the focus has included achievement data these contain various levels of analysis of students' achievement compared with standards that have been discussed and agreed with partners, typically national norms and curriculum levels. Such analyses are undertaken for all schools in the cluster, for individual schools and across subgroups of interest (e.g. gender, ethnicity and starting achievement level). These reports become the grounds for and focus of the collaborative meaning making with partners in PLCs and are designed to build the partners' capability in collaborative analysis of data. Through these artefacts, we aim to influence how partners think about their current data and to influence their future data gathering and analysis by modelling the practices of gathering, analysing and interpreting data.

The second primary artefacts are analyses of teaching and/or school practice systematically linked with the student learning outcomes, for example teaching practices associated with achievement patterns identified in the student achievement artefacts. The purpose of these artefacts is to influence how partners' think about their current teaching and school data in relation to valued learning outcomes, and again, to model the practices of gathering, analysing and interpreting similar data in future. This analysis of teaching can be in the form of excerpts of transcripts from classrooms that illustrate effective practices related to the research literature (e.g. transcripts of a portion of a lesson where the teacher has an extended discussion with her students about the meaning of a word). These excerpts exemplify how to enact effective practices in the classroom, and also become the basis for discussing other, similar effective practices that might be used. Artefacts can also be in the form of case studies of a teacher's or school's practices, for example, a transcript of a lesson or a written case study of a school has achieved accelerated achievement gains.

Another type of teaching practice artefact is a written report or PowerPoint that shows the absence or presence of features of teaching practice at cluster (i.e. across all schools in an intervention) and school level analysed quantitatively, for example, the number of open questions asked by a teacher. This provides information on whether the features of teaching determined through a combination of research literature and the local context are present or absent in a classroom.

The function and the specific content of the two sets of artefacts differ within and across phases. At the start of Phase 1, the function of the artefacts is to support the partners identify the nature and extent of the problem, and to test hypotheses for the reasons for the problem. So the content of the artefacts focus on student learning outcomes (the typical valued student outcome in our work) and on the strengths and weaknesses of students in these outcomes in relation to the agreed point of comparison. For achievement this is often the rates of gain, levels and distributions of achievement compared with national norms, and on teaching and school practices that could explain the patterns of achievement, such as the transcripts of teaching practice. In the first phase, there is usually more extensive and intensive data collection and analysis of student learning to contextualise effective practice to local contexts. So the content of artefacts sometimes include other kinds of data such as school or parent data that are hypothesised to impact on the valued outcomes (e.g. parents' perceptions of the value of secondary school qualifications). At the end of Phase 1, the function of the artefact is to support partners understand the impact of the changes to practice undertaken in Phase 1 and typically are reports on achievement data (as that is typically the valued outcome) to test whether achievement has improved as planned. Artefacts on teaching such as a report on the changes to teaching practice that are hypothesised to be related to patterns in student data are also used to support partners understand the changes in achievement in relation to their hypotheses. In subsequent Phases, each beginning and end of year artefact focusses on the changes in, for example, achievement and practice for that year and identifies areas that might result in a re-design. Especially for analyses of achievement, the start of year artefacts also examine whether achievement has dropped over the summer holidays.

There is always support to engage with, understand and use the artefacts, to develop a shared understanding of the purpose and use of the artefact. We provide notes about how to read data representations in many of our written reports, and amplify this in our face-to-face discussions of data in PLCs. In recent years, we have added online resources to support the understanding of these artefacts, for example, videos to support school leaders and teachers 'read' the data such as how to understand the differences between box and whisker graphs. We do this with the intent that teachers and leaders not only develop a nuanced understanding of the specific data and evidence we present but that they learn how to collect, analyse, interpret and use similar data and evidence themselves in the future.

Caveat

LSM applications to date have typically been situated within a content-area (e.g., literacy) where an issue with student learning in the content-area has been the motivation for starting the LSM intervention and where the valued student outcomes are generally framed in terms of improvement in literacy outcomes. As such the focus of the research is constrained by content-area knowledge in literacy, and the structure of the content-area becomes a theoretical guide, albeit we have also examined non-literacy issues that might impact on outcomes such as student retention. Moreover, in our investigation of student profiles, literacy issues are often implicated more strongly as influencing student outcomes than other non-literacy issues. Thus, in our work, because of the expertise of the research team, the shared literacy outcome focus and the profiles of student learning, much of the contextualisation and problem solution focus in the collaborative analysis of data has been on developing literacy instruction in the classroom. If the presenting problem with student learning is situated in another content-area, then that content-area would guide the analysis of the data. The content-area would also guide the composition of the research team, and recent applications in different content-areas have resulted in different compositions of research team members. For example, when mathematics has been a focus, we have included a content-area expert in mathematics in the research team.

It is the onus of the researcher to more than simply acknowledge any identified caveats as influencing variables, but to develop methodologically robust ways to demonstrate that that their hypotheses and solutions through the collaborative analysis process is defendable, and that alternate hypotheses and solutions are acknowledged, and if possible tested and discounted. We have described in this chapter and throughout this book various systematic processes for doing so. For example: an agreed evaluation criteria for testing and confirming hypotheses and solutions using evidence described here and in Chapter Two, and checks on the effectiveness of proposed solutions in every phase through the analysis of data (see also Chapter One). We also describe these processes more fully in specific publications relating to our projects such as Lai, McNaughton, Amituanai-Toloa, et al. (2009).

Chapter Four

Partnerships for Design and Sustainability

Partnerships are at the heart of design-based approaches like the LSM. Yet, as we argued in Chapter One, far less attention has been given to how to develop partnerships in pragmatic, principled and theory-informed ways. In this chapter, we exemplify the LSM partnership approach with a focus on a key function of the partnership with schools that is to co-design solutions to identified problems. As LSM applications typically focus on improving student learning, here we focus on the co-design and implementation of an intervention in an area of student learning that is contextually appropriate. We use the term 'intervention' to signal that the co-designed solution is intended to affect changes in the typical class-room or school practice. As discussed in previous chapters, such co-design focuses on strengthening school and classroom practice based on shared hypotheses that emerge from the evidence of the pattern of teaching and learning, and the relation-ships between the two. Negotiated refinements to existing practice are designed to address identified learning challenges. These processes of co-design draw on prac-tice knowledge as well as research expertise, and purposefully embed each LSM application within a context, making it meaningful to teachers and leaders.

We illustrate how the partnership approach is woven into the LSM in ways that develop a targeted intervention that is theoretically robust, locally relevant and practically achievable. The process of co-design is a form of professional learning for schools and supports the sustainability of the intervention, two other key functions of the partnerships. In the first section, we summarise the purposes and roles within an LSM partnership. While the partnership can have different features in different contexts, we work to maintain the integrity of the core fea-tures of a partnership. The collaborative analysis of data in PLCs underpins the LSM and is integral to partnerships, and we explain the structure of, and roles of partners in, the PLCs. Finally, we discuss the knowledge and skills required to function effectively as partners.

Partnerships reflect each context and we use two contrasting examples to illustrate this. The first, which we will call, the Digital Schools Partnership is an enduring and evolving long-term partnership with initially 7 (then 12, and even-tually 84) schools that implemented an ubiquitous digital teaching and learning platform within their face-to-face classes. These schools all serve culturally and

Research-practice Partnerships for School Improvement:
The Learning Schools Model, 57–71

linguistically diverse urban low socio-economic communities in NZ and were focussed on improving writing in the first instance. The second example, which we will call the Pacific Literacy partnership with three Pacific Island nations was developed as part of a consortium of institutions from NZ and these nations. In each country, the profiling indicated different focus areas: writing, reading comprehension and meaning-making using language and texts. Fifteen schools in each country worked in clusters, largely formed around geographic proximity. In each country one coordinator provided overall coordination of activities in-country as well as led literacy activities.

Partnership Purposes and Roles: Why Collaborate?

In the first three chapters we outlined the importance of partnerships in achieving the twin goals of advancing knowledge while improving pressing problems of practice. The goal of the partnership is twofold: to co-design an intervention that is contextualised to the local contexts, and to learn how to improve that design through iterative cycles of analysing data. A key role for researchers within the partnership is to contribute research knowledge to support this co-design and learning though the iterative cycles of collaborative analysis of data. The school professionals' role is to contribute knowledge and expertise towards that co-design, and also engage in the formulating and testing of best fit hypotheses. Through the ongoing dialogue, across multiple school sites and at different levels of leadership, school leaders, teachers and researchers work together to develop context-appropriate instructional designs. School leaders and teachers test these to consider how they work and for whom (Cobb, Confrey, diSessa, Lehrer, & Schauble, 2003) through practical use in classrooms. As with 'lesson study' (Fernandez & Yoshida, 2012) approaches, the responsibility for the design of new practices is shared, and therefore there is collective responsibility for effectiveness. Research data and practitioner experiences both contribute evidence for the evaluation of effectiveness of the new designs and subsequent refinements.

To design an intervention that is at once theoretically strong and contextually strong, it stands to reason that the partnership needs to incorporate people who have strong academic knowledge of the issue at hand (typically researchers); alongside people who know well the context, the students and their communities (typically school leaders and teachers). This increases the depth and breadth of knowledge available for co-design, and strengthens and critiques existing practices. This conception of the partnership signifies a departure from the situation where researchers design and deliver a set of instructional procedures, and therefore is different from what might be initially expected of researchers by prospective partners in an intervention.

A second purpose of partnering to co-design an intervention is to build teacher and school leader capability. Done well, the collaborative analysis of data processes for intervention co-design where teachers and leaders in schools collect, analyse and review data about learning and teaching with research partners over successive cycles enable a school ultimately to be able to self-improve

(Bryk et al., 2015), or, in our terms, to become a 'Learning School'. Through participation in these processes with partners, teachers and leaders build the sorts of expertise to enable this. Skills such as the defining of target areas for improvement, identifying and designing instructional responses that might support that improvement, noticing and recognising learning processes, positing hypotheses, positing alternative hypotheses, identifying barriers and supporting colleagues to change are all embedded within the partnership work. Through participation in these sorts of conversations, content knowledge as well as knowledge of processes for improvement, both grow. Developing content knowledge and knowledge of the improvement process in teachers and schools' own context have been found to be effective in supporting teachers and schools' learning. Researchers have learnt, for example, that involving teachers in their own setting supported them understand the relevance of the intervention in particular the research components of the intervention, and increased their desire to participate (Coburn, Penuel, & Geil, 2013).

For any intervention to be sustainable, partners must share an understanding of improvement processes, as well as implement practices. The partnership for the LSM is therefore designed to build capability in leading these improvement processes within schools, enabling responsibility for maintaining the ongoing improvement processes to shift from researchers to the schools.

Principles of Partnerships

Collaborating with partners can be difficult, complex and time-consuming. It is also not well taught in higher education institutions (Snow, 2015). Building partnerships effectively requires researchers to understand the theory, principles and pragmatics of how to conduct partnerships across cultures and languages, and in different situations. A number of research theories of partnerships could achieve these aims. Given that collaborative analysis of data for co-design is a key focus of the partnership, our focus is on partnerships that are underlined by data based discussions in ill-structured problems; the solutions to which are 'high stakes' in the sense that they matter for students, teachers, leaders and communities.

Our approach to these charged discussions is consistent in many ways with the conversation principles in theories of action (Argyris, 1982), and in problem-based methodology (Robinson & Lai, 2006) which have been refined by Robinson and are now known as Open-to-learning Conversations TM. The LSM principles are also consistent with those of effective PLCs and professional learning networks (e.g. Bolam, McMahon, Stoll, Thomas, & Wallace, 2005). The key principle and the foundation for all discussions is rigour with respect – rigour in the analysis and interrogation of the data, hypotheses and solutions, and respect for the knowledge and perspectives of others in the community (Robinson & Lai, 2006). A wider concern around the lack of rigour in applied educational research (Snow, 2015) suggests a strong focus is needed on the former aspect.

The dual focus on rigour and respect addresses two well-known risks in partnerships. A focus solely on rigour carries the risk that interrogating the data is done with little regard to the feelings of the partners, with the consequence that partners lose motivation or feel less efficacious, and this in turns leads partners to not engage fully in the intervention. A focus on rigour alone fails to understand or address the human conditions that shape and influence the success of any partnership. A second risk is to be rigorous with the analysis and use of data, but to avoid challenging conversations and weaken the message because of a concern that the partners might be angry or upset with the message. This lacks a different more social and respectful rigour necessary for partnerships to make an impact on practice. The result may be peaceful, but dishonest (and ultimately less respectful) relationships, where what is known by one partner is not disclosed to the other but is often talked about behind the partners' back. A quote from a school leader in the first LSM application captures the challenges of being both respectful and rigorous

> In order for teachers to engage in meaningful discussion about student achievement data, we need to build relationships among teachers so that these discussions will focus on how to examine the data to improve teaching, rather than blaming someone or excusing the poor results. (Robinson & Lai, 2006, p. 36)

In conversations, the respectful focus is on learning from each other's views, rather than on trying to impose one's view on another, and treating differences in perspective as opportunities to learn rather than opportunities to persuade or obstacles to be overcome. These dispositions to knowledge building from multiple perspectives underpin the strength that is inherent in a partnership approach that respects various sorts of expertise. A knowledge building disposition is vital in collaborative analysis of data and co-design, as there are often differences between partners such as around the locus of the problem (e.g. schools, parents and government policies) or around the solutions to address the problem (e.g. preferred theories and solutions). Rather than have conversations that focus on control and coercion of others to adopt one's views, the focus is on learning about the various views and then checking the validity and applicability of these views.

Respectful discussions also need to be rigorous, and in the case of the LSM, there are agreed evaluation criteria and/or principles that can be used to evaluate the content of the discussions (see Chapter Three). For example, when collaboratively discussing data with the schools, it is important to be clear about student's position in comparison to national averages. If we soften this message, partners may not realise how poorly their students are performing and may not view students' performance to be a problem; in which case we would not be able to make an impact because there would be no agreement on the problem to be solved. However, rather than dismiss these reactions to the data, we use these as the opportunity to discuss and jointly develop hypotheses to be tested. In our LSM applications, some teachers and school leaders' theories such as students' having strong decoding skills were borne out by the data, but others such as lack of breakfast being an issue were not. Some researcher theories have been borne out by the data such as the lack of checking of evidence from text, but others such as the need for direct instruction of literacy strategies were not. We, as researchers, have also proposed hypotheses that have turned out to be unsupportable, or have reacted to data in a way that tried to protect researchers' positions. An example of the latter occurred in the middle of an application where the school leaders wanted to change the standardised reading assessment arguing that an equally psychometrically robust alternative would be more reliably used by teachers. In order to protect the repeated measurement in the quasi-experimental design we resisted, but ultimately realised that we could transform data to accommodate the need and in so doing also check inter-comparability. Through this process, researchers, school leaders and teachers came to a deeper understanding of contextually appropriate assessments than we could have done without being both respectful yet rigorous.

Respect and rigour have local variations, and thus need to be contextually appropriate. Contextual appropriateness here means being respectful and rigorous in a way that is appropriate to the history within the schools and cultures of those we are partnering with, including how leaders enact their roles which can have different characteristics in different cultural settings. That is, respect and rigour is necessary but insufficient to enable us to be effective partners. We often work in cultures not our own, and this requires cultural expertise (discussed in the final section of this chapter). This also requires what is often called 'soft skills' (but are actually very hard skills!), and in Chapter Seven, we discuss how to reason using these so-called 'soft skills' and what we have learnt about doing so in a respectful and rigorous way.

Professional Learning Communities (PLCs)

The sites for collaborative analyses, where the partnerships are enacted, are PLCs within a school or across schools. These are planned communities that align with the purposes of a specific LSM application and are integrated within normal school or cluster (across school) business. There is agreement on the number and function of these communities established with school leaders prior to each year of the LSM. There is agreement on the multiple functions such as knowledge building or intervention design and redesign. Normal school business means that the PLCs are well integrated with the wider school communities and what is undertaken with the application of the LSM becomes what the school normally does. In this way, the application is not seen as an extra from the start, but part of the schools' core business. Here we discuss how PLCs are set up before summarising the sites and structures that are common across all applications and what we have found to be critical in establishing these communities.

PLC Setup

It is worth pointing out that we do not start the partnerships at the point of the collaborative analysis of data with the key school leaders in the school communities. Before any such conversations, in the initial stages of the partnership, it is important to have a shared understanding of what counts as valued student outcomes. If the shared valued outcome is about student achievement, then there needs to be shared understanding of what assessments or tools are best placed to measure those outcomes. This can involve several rounds of discussions, and typically includes both discussions around school and community aspirations for their students and discussions about possible assessment, measures and/or tools, including their strengths and weaknesses and how they relate to the valued student outcomes. At the outset, it is also important to make clear the formative rationale for the collection of any student achievement data, if this is the focus, and provide assurance of anonymity of schools, teachers and students. Our experience, especially in larger scale applications using achievement data where there is potential for multiple partners to hold different interpretations, it is vital that schools and their communities see the collection and analysis of student achievement data as crucial to their own purposes. Any suspicion that the data will be used to report about school or teacher effectiveness for external accountability purposes, we have found to be a threat to authentic partnership, and therefore a threat to ongoing engagement with the processes of change.

Another aspect of our work which reduces such threat is how we evaluate the effects of what is implemented to improve teaching practices. Given our conception of partnership, the researchers' role is not to evaluate the 'quality' of *individual* teachers against a preset set of effectiveness criteria. Accountability or appraisal are functions that undermine the partnership because they change the balance of power and confuse functions. The context-embedded instructional design and the ongoing development of improvable instructional approaches would be compromised by including an accountability or appraisal function. Instead, teacher review and accountability are considered to be the school's role; the researchers' is to describe, as closely as possible, the current state of affairs as *patterns* of practice, so that with schools, partners might consider evidence and posit *collective* refinements. So, despite the fact that researchers will often be in teachers' classes, watching their teaching, teacher performance review is not part of the research conversation, instead the conversations focuses on instructional co-design improvement to meet the needs of students. This is a point about role clarity that we have found is worth making explicitly at the outset of any partnership. Any evaluation, as we stated earlier in previous chapters, is focussed on the *quality* of the hypotheses and solutions to the hypotheses, rather than the on appraisal of individual teacher's practices.

Commonly, a breakthrough in trust occurs between the partners after initial conversations around patterns of teaching and learning and the hypothesised relationships between the two. In other words, we do not expect full trust at the start, but trust sufficient to agree on the purposes of collecting the data. It is through the PLC conversations that the breakthrough occurs. This is because the process develops shared understanding of the problem and its solution in a way that respects yet tests both research and school leaders and teachers' theories.

Structure and Focus

Various within-school and across-school groups are sites for PLCs associated with an application of LSM. Researchers, as part of the partnership, typically join across-schools PLCs comprised of school leaders and participate in multiple PLCs both within and across schools early on in an LSM application to set up the partnership, contribute to the collaborative analysis of data, and co-design specific interventions within the partnership. In some applications, there have been PLCs co-led by researchers usually for a limited time to build school capacity, and there have also been instances where there has been a specific request for researchers to join a within-school PLC to help build capability. However, researcher involvement is flexible and dependent on context.

Flexible engagement by researchers, school leaders and teachers in within- and across-school sites is characteristic of each application of the LSM. A concept that has contributed to our thinking around flexible engagement using indigenous Māori theorising (Kaupapa Māori principles) is a whānau (extended family) of interest (Smith, 1999), where researchers and educators with their local communities function like an extended family. The metaphor draws attention to the reciprocal obligations, rights and roles that are similar to those operating in an extended family. Just as each extended family dynamic is different, each PLC set up across applications of the LSM is different and based on the 'family relationship' in each context. In what follows, we discuss the typical within- and across-school sites, with a focus on school leaders' and teachers' roles.

Within-Schools Sites

Existing school meetings are the typical sites within schools for PLCs to collaboratively analyse data (e.g. Lai, McNaughton, Timperley, et al., 2009). Schools use a variety of staff and team meetings for these purposes. This is to ensure that every teacher and leader in the school belongs to at least one school PLC to collaboratively analyse data. For example, a principal might belong to a PLC with his or her senior leaders to collaboratively analyse school data, as well as belong to a PLC involving all staff where the school-wide data are discussed.

Each within-school PLC has a designated leader who holds either a formal position within a school (e.g. Principal and team leader) or an informal leader. Typically, all school leaders with formal roles belong to at least one community, and take a leadership role in that community or in other communities. Leaders tend to be the ones that were originally responsible for the school meeting that has now been turned into a meeting involving collaborative analysis of data.

Researchers on occasion join the within-school PLCs, but these are typically during the first year to set up the partnership and discuss the profiles of data which forms the basis of the partnership, or when invited to support the knowledge building in a particular community.

Across-School Sites

Across-school sites either use an existing across-school structure if one had existed prior to the LSM commencing (Lai & McNaughton, 2018), or one is negotiated and established at the start of each LSM application. These can be primarily face-to-face, or a combination of face-to-face and online (Lai et al., 2014).

The membership of these are typically leaders or school representatives that are tasked with learning from the across-school communities, and tasked with taking the learning back into their individual schools (Lai & McNaughton, 2018). At least twice a year for the duration of the LSM, the researchers meet with key people in the schools to discuss collaboratively the emerging evidence across the schools and in individual schools, where appropriate. However, the number and structure of meetings responds to the contextual needs and opportunities and the characteristics of the particular whānau (extended family) of interest.

The focus of the collaborative analysis in these communities varies according to where in the analysis process the LSM application is at. For example, at the start of the school year the focus is on analysing patterns of achievement from recently collected achievement data, and on discussing the implications for practice. Meetings during the year focus on developing and monitoring the impact of the changes on practice, and meetings at the end of the year and sometimes at the beginning of the year evaluate the impact of the changes in practice.

Table 1 offers an example of the various PLCs that operated as core business within one cluster of schools. Participants worked in horizontal across-school and vertical within-school PLCs with various purposes. All schools in the cluster sent representatives to the 'hui' each year, where teachers, researchers and school leaders presented evidence of changes and challenges. (A hui is an indigenous Māori word for gathering used in NZ.) In addition, Principals worked as a group using data for planning and direction setting, and researchers were invited to these meetings to discuss research evidence and directions. Middle leaders also met once every term to consider research evidence and engage in professional learning. Researchers attended these meetings to support teacher PLD, if needed (but other times, expertise could be found in the schools or nearby). Traditional school structures, such as staff meetings and team meetings, were also used for PLC activities.

Research into the PLCs

A set of factors have emerged from our work as necessary conditions in the effective functioning of PLCs. These are similar to what others have found. Firstly, coherence across communities through a common purpose and common collaborative processes is important. We have found that schools that sustained achievement gains and continued collaborative analysis of data had developed an explicit and shared goal able that was articulated at all levels in the school (Lai & McNaughton, 2018). This is similar to findings on instructional programme coherence that has been implicated in schools that make greater gains in achievement (e.g. Newmann, Smith, Allensworth, & Bryk, 2001).

A second factor is the role of school leaders in maintaining and sustaining PLCs. In our studies of LSM applications (e.g. Lai & McNaughton, 2018), leaders demonstrate the known characteristics of effective leadership such as instructional leadership through their leading of PLCs. This is also the leadership characteristic identified as having the most impact on achievement (see Robinson, Lloyd, & Rowe, 2008). Other leadership characteristics identified as

Table 1. Digital Schools Partnership PLC Structures.

Group	Participants	Purpose	Activities	Artefacts	Timing
Whole cluster (across-school) staff meeting	All staff from all schools Researchers	Provide research feedback about the cluster as a whole to all teachers and leaders	Presentation and discussion of student achievement and teaching data patterns at cluster level up to the end of the previous school year. Discussions for formative evaluation and reflection, hypothesis generation and preliminary goal setting	Data presentation on student achievement and teaching data patterns at cluster level	Yearly (February)
Principals' PLC	Principals of all schools Researchers (when invited, at least twice a year but typically more often)	Principal learning, cluster and school coherence, strategic direction	Presentation and discussion of student achievement and teaching data patterns at cluster and school level, principal knowledge sharing, cluster planning	School and cluster student achievement data, classroom observation analyses cluster plans, research presentations, milestone reports	Two full PLC days in addition to four regular meetings per year
School Leaders' PLC	Deputy and Associate Principals or Curriculum leaders (including year level and/or learning area leaders) Researchers	Leader learning, dissemination to and discussion with teachers, cross school collaboration, feedback from leaders about activities in their schools	Presentation and discussion of student achievement and teaching data patterns at school level	School achievement and progress data, research milestone reports, classroom observation analyses	Termly (four per year)

Table 1. (*Continued*)

Group	Participants	Purpose	Activities	Artefacts	Timing
Whole cluster hui	School leadership teams, representative teachers from each school, parent representatives, philanthropic funders, student representatives, researchers	Coherence across the cluster, identifying innovation and positive deviance, review and forward planning	Feedback (using data) from students, teachers and researchers	Student, teacher and researcher presentations	Yearly (August)
School PLCs	School staff	Implementation, pedagogical shift	Presentation and discussion of student achievement and teaching data patterns at school level, knowledge building, Professional Learning and Development	Targeted professional learning, school achievement data	Varies by school – typically twice termly (8 per year)
Team PLCs	Teaching teams	Planning and evaluation of practice	Presentation and discussion of student achievement and teaching data patterns at team level, Planning, shared problem solving	Team-level achievement data, class and team sites	Typically fortnightly

Source: Adapted from Jesson, McNaughton, Wilson et al. (2018, Table 1).

important, including embedding communities into the school's normal routines and championing these communities, are also consistent with other studies on the characteristics of effective PLCs (e.g. Bolam et al., 2005).

Two further factors may have played an important role in the effectiveness of these PLCs: the pre-history of teachers and school leaders working in communities, and the educational policy context of NZ. In many applications, there have been networks of within-school and across-school meetings that were sites for previous school improvement initiatives. Applications of LSM capitalised on this pre-history drawing on the infrastructure of existing meetings and where possible skills and knowledge associated with the capability to be a partner in the LSM. Moreover, the NZ Ministry of Education has supported and continues to support collaborative work. For example, a current Ministry initiative brings together education and training providers (e.g. early learning, post-secondary) to work together to solve a shared goal or achievement challenge based on the particular needs facing its children and young people (Ministry of Education, n.d.-c) However, neither condition are deal breakers. In the Pacific Literacy Partnership, for example, no such communities existed. We therefore worked with participating schools to establish these, and develop expectations for how they would become embedded in school business as usual, without interrupting the teaching and learning.

Knowledge and Skills for Collaboration

To design an intervention that is at once theoretically strong and contextually strong, the partnership needs to have people who have strong academic or research knowledge of the issue at hand; alongside people who know well the context, the students and their communities. In general at least several sets of skills and knowledge contribute to the expertise necessary for an effective PLC of the sort we described here. An important principle across these sets is that an effective PLCs in any application of the LSM requires well developed skills related to processes (e.g. data analysis) as well as to content (e.g. content-area knowledge).

Skill Set 1: Teaching Expertise and PCK

At the most generic level, the focus of an application of the LSM is to support schools to be more effective. This typically means developing improved instructional designs that meet identified needs; and this in turn requires teaching expertise based on strong PCK (Shulman, 1986). PCK, as we briefly explained before, comprises both knowledge of the subject or content-area and how to teach it. Content-area knowledge is knowledge of how the content-area area is structured, its progressions and outcomes. It is knowledge of the technical concepts, methods and principles that define the content-area such as in history, literacy or biology. In the PCK Shulman (1986) described, experts know how to adapt content to specific patterns of students' errors or misconceptions, they know how lessons need to flow, for how long and how often. They know where emphasis will need to be placed, which resources will be likely to support students and so on. They also know patterns of students, what parents expect and how new ideas can be embedded into existing routines that work.

Such skills and knowledge can reside across different PLC participants, and can be within schools or within the research community and other partners. In collaborative analysis of data, each partner brings their respective expert knowledge of teaching to the PLC to co-design the intervention. For example, in the Digital Schools Partnership, teaching expertise sat at multiple levels within the cluster of schools. Many school principals were teaching experts, as were many school curriculum leaders, team leaders and teachers. But the profile of teaching expertise varied between teachers. Close analysis of teachers also suggested that teachers themselves had a range of expertise: some stronger at leading students in conversations that challenged thinking, others more expert in planning and with designing activities to build independence; others had highly responsive interactions with students, others provided high-level textual support and so forth. Rarely is there a teacher who perfectly enacts all parts of the highly complex craft that is teaching. Instead, each of the experts offered a resource for others to call on for support. In this application, teachers' blogs, and class websites were shared between teachers as resources to capitalise on the distributed expertise. PLCs operated for teachers, school leaders and researchers to share expertise and ideas and research feedback and discussion were all sites where teaching expertise was acknowledged and made visible.

Skill Set 2: Research Knowledge

The people with theoretical expertise, typically the research partners, bring underlying educational research and learning theories, as well as a knowledge about international and national interventions and research that has previously been shown to be effective within a particular content-area or that can be applied to that content-area. While research has demonstrated that certain approaches are likely to be effective, skills are needed to analyse the instructional designs already in place or which could be put in place from an explanatory, rather than descriptive point of view. This is typically part of the process of contextualising of effective practice to local contexts, and learning from variability in the system (See Chapters One and Two).

The value of such explanatory analysis for practice is firstly to understand why something is working or not and under what condition and for whom does it work, rather than to simply describe what is the case with little explanation of why it is effective or not. Without an understanding of the explanatory value of a practice, it is possible to focus on extraneous features of the practice that in turn leads to little to no change in intended outcomes when adopted by others. Within the Digital Schools partnership, for example, researchers analysed the teachers' websites and students' blogs to understand practices that worked, and accompanied this with annotated theory about why these observed practices were likely to be effective. These analyses offered resources for teachers and leaders with which to further change practice.

Skill Set 3: Leadership

At different levels in a cluster of schools, leaders play an enabling, supporting and insisting role. We have found leaders to be another necessary factor in effectively functioning communities, both during and after an LSM application (see Chapter Six). Leaders are those who hold formal leadership roles (e.g. principals) and those who enact leadership functions without a formal role. Leaders work as the change managers, to resource coherent changes in school routines and in teachers' repertoires of practice. They support the sites for conversations, give time appropriately for people in schools to make changes, they put systems in place for the collection and moderation of data about learning and teaching, they lead conversations to build coherence of vision throughout a school, they support and offer opportunities for shared reflection. Leaders can support the success of any intervention through their attention and presence as instructional leaders, or conversely, undo it through apathy or absence. They have an advocacy function too as demonstrated in highly effective intervention programmes (May, Sirinides, Gray, & Goldsworthy, 2016).

Leaders are also pivotal at marshalling community expertise: those who know and represent the values and aspirations of the community, as well as appreciate and can draw from the strengths already working within a community. In the Pacific Literacy Partnership school leaders held community meetings about the proposed changes within the schools and sought community input into the shape of those changes. Moreover, the meetings became sites for parents to see the sorts of professional learning that the teachers were engaging in; an activity that school leaders believed lifted the professional standing of the school in the community.

Leadership expertise can vary within and between schools, and this variation changes how the partnership is developed across different LSM contexts. In the Pacific Literacy partnership, for example, school leadership that focussed on student and teacher learning was an explicit focus for development. So, in this partnership, the Centre for Educational Leadership at the University of Auckland (https://www.uacel.ac.nz/) was a key partner in building leadership expertise to enable the school based professional learning required within the partnership. In the Digital Schools Partnership, school leaders, who like teachers have varying styles and strengths, met as a regular PLC to work together to drive the sorts of changes agreed upon for collective improvement.

Skill Set 4: Analysis and Use of Data

The partnership includes people who have expertise in analysing and using data to raise and test hypotheses and develop solutions. At the beginning, these skills and knowledge are likely more often part of the repertoire of the researchers but also within some schools and some teachers. These team members bring skills of analysis, and processes for understanding the data such as variation and variability, leading the use of data to find what works well, under what conditions, how often, how much and how fast. These PLC members serve to draw associations between the sorts of teaching and school practices observed and the outcomes achieved, as well as fine-tune the discussion to differing parts of the issue (see the extended example in Chapter Three).

Chapter Three elaborates on the collaborative analysis of data processes in detail and focuses on the collection of teaching and student achievement data. However, here, we wish to point out that the skills and knowledge-based required are not just to analyse the data and to interpret and understand patterns, but also to create tools or artefacts to collect data. One LSM application involved researchers working with teachers to design a classroom observation tool that included categorisation of what students were spending time doing in class (e.g. reading, writing, spelling and so forth). Included in the categorisation was whether the child was 'on task' or 'off task'. Closer analyses revealed that many off-task children were unable to be on task, because they were waiting for some direction of what to do, or waiting for the resources necessary for an activity. This lead teachers and leaders to consider the amount of time spent waiting in a class, the reasons for waiting, and the lesson planning required so that children's time is well used.

Skill Set 5: Deliberate Dialogue and Facilitation

Experience suggests that not all people with content-area expertise or expertise in analysing data are strong at working with large groups of adults in challenging conversations. Thus, the fifth type of expertise needed within the partners is what we call 'facilitation'; skills in leading conversations about challenging subjects, often student achievement and its relationship to the teaching. Without such skills, it would be difficult to enact the 'collaboration' component of collaborative analysis of data so central to the LSM. We have already described some important processes for collaboratively analysing data, such as undertaking those with rigour and respect and the use of evaluation criteria to evaluate hypotheses and their possible solutions. Such expertise can reside in researcher or school partners. However, as the focus of leading conversations is collaborative analysis of data, this requires an integration of knowledge and skills in both leading conversations and analysis of data. Typically research partners have this combination of skills and knowledge. So here, we focus on the aspects of leading conversation that researchers need in order to be successful based on our work.

Researchers need to have well-developed skills for communicating with schools, presenting, and speaking the language of schools. This is one part of the translation problem reported in Chapter One and also identified by others (Snow, 2015), such as where researchers need to translate what is often academic jargon into 'teacher speak' without losing the rigour of the original. Researchers also need to know how to translate from theory to practice, that is to either demonstrate how the theoretical ideas can be used in practice, and/or to facilitate the conversation such that school partners understand how to do so themselves. In practice, such skills mean that teachers see the value of the process; they get teachers and leaders to the table and they keep them there. The partnership is central to this process, in that the research partners need to be, and be seen to be, supportive and respectful of the difficult work that teachers and school leaders engage in every day. In the Digital Schools Partnership, a team of facilitators worked with the schools to collect student achievement data, oversee reliability and moderation processes where necessary, observe in classes, lead PLCs focussed on collaboratively analysing data, and support schools to use the data for their own reporting or meaning-making. In the Pacific Literacy Partnership, facilitators based in NZ took on this function and supported in-country facilitators to do the same. These people were the key research-practice connection and had high levels of pedagogical expertise as well as an emerging research capability that was strengthened through the partnership.

Skill Set 6: Cultural Expertise

All people are culturally located. In NZ, for example, culturally sustaining pedagogies are increasing recognised as being those that uphold the principles of interdependence and partnership enshrined within the Treaty of Waitangi, the founding national document. Berryman, Lawrence, and Lamont (2018) describes such partnerships and relationships as having 'mana orite': within which power is shared, culture counts, learning is interactive and dialogic, connectedness is fundamental to relations and there is a common vision of excellence for Māori in education. Similarly in educational research, the processes need to be those of partnership which involves working with participants in a dialogic and responsive manner (Bishop, 2011). While each of us likes to think that this is how we work, and it is certainly what we aim to achieve, specific cultural contexts have differing tacit norms of interaction, and specific actions or contributions can be construed in unintended ways. For this reason, when the research partners are working in an unfamiliar cultural setting, cultural expertise is an important consideration.

When we have worked in different cultural contexts, our approach has been to acknowledge the cultural expertise, and to build this into the partnership. Modes of discourse vary across cultures. In Pacific cultures, for example, Talanoa (Vaioleti, 2006) or storytelling surrounding important issues might seem to the outsider to be about everyday occurrences, but contain important abstract ideas to be conveyed. In the Solomon Islands context, Tok-stori (Sanga, Reynolds, & Paulsen, 2018) is the means of gathering and making sense of experiences as well as a process for change. Cultural experts, typically from the schools or wider community, or in some instances other researchers in the same institution, help the researchers navigate the differences in interactional expectations. In some settings where we have worked, for example, respect will mean a more indirect discussion of theories and a more implicit critique of practice, possibly through story. In one example, criticism of an approach was conveyed through a story showing criticism of oneself using that approach. In another example, a member of the wider team had to be taught explicitly about how to 'read the silence' in teachers' response. While the specifics of cultural expertise vary across contexts, the principles hold true: cultural expertise is both important and necessary.

Chapter Five

Resourcing and Professional Learning and Development (PLD)

In this chapter, we focus on resourcing to solve the shared problems identified through previous phases, where resourcing includes all actions taken to build on strengths and to address identified needs. The most common form of resourcing in our applications of the LSM has been the provision of teacher and leader PLD opportunities designed to build on identified strengths and to address identified gaps in instruction and leadership. The goal in this case is to positively impact on prioritised and agreed problems of student learning through improvements in teaching and school practice. But resourcing is not limited to PLD and could also include provision of specialist staff, the development of new infrastructure (such as IT infrastructure) and the development of texts or other learning resources. The content and provision of resources in a particular application are always bespoke as they are designed and tailored to the particular profile of strengths and needs developed in Phase 1: Profiling.

Although we will discuss examples of other forms of resources we have implemented in Phase 2: Resourcing, this chapter focusses mainly on the design and provision of PLD to improve teaching practices, including instruction in the classroom and the practices that impact on that instruction such as teacher planning and reflection. So first we explain why PLD is at the very heart of all phases of the LSM, with a particular focus on PLD in the second, resourcing phase. We discuss key principles underpinning our PLD approach with illustrations from different applications of the LSM and we discuss the tensions of using a bespoke model of PLD which is developed through the process of contextualising effective practice to local contexts. Similarly, we describe and then discuss the tensions in using a cascade structure of PLD. We end by briefly discussing other forms of resourcing used in LSM studies.

In previous chapters, we have discussed the kinds of knowledge that are important to the LSM processes, and which are developed through the LSM. So we will not revisit this material again, except to note the following: Firstly, as others have long intimated (e.g. Kennedy, 1998) what is learnt, that is the content of the resourcing, is as important as how it is learnt. Secondly, as implied in earlier

Research-practice Partnerships for School Improvement:
The Learning Schools Model, 73–86
Copyright © 2020 by Mei Kuin Lai, Stuart McNaughton, Rebecca Jesson and Aaron Wilson
Published under exclusive license
doi:10.1108/978-1-78973-571-020201006

chapters, that knowledge building in the LSM seeks to build both knowledge of the specific shared problem and how to solve it, as well as generative knowledge and skills (e.g. collaborative analysis of data) that can be applied to solve similar and dissimilar issues in in the future. In this way, knowledge building through resourcing has both an immediate focus and a future focus.

Why Focus on PLD to Improve Teaching Practices?

The main reason we focus on improving teaching as a lever of change is because the ultimate goal of LSM is almost always to positively impact on prioritised problems of valued student learning, and research evidence suggests that teaching is the most influential of all within system factors on student learning (see meta-analysis by Hattie, 2009). Such evidence is supported empirically through repeated applications of the LSM with a teacher PLD focus that show consistent improvements in valued student achievement outcomes as a result of a focus on fine tuning and thereby improving teaching practices (see Chapter One). Although our LSM applications also typically focus on developing leadership, we do so in order that leaders can more effectively influence teachers who have a more direct influence on student learning. In this way, the focus is always on improving teaching.

What we also know through the research evidence and through successive LSM applications is that the knowledge and skills required to enact the LSM to improve teaching and learning are complex and not typically part of a teacher's or school leader's existing repertoire. For example, collaborative analysis of data is at the heart of every LSM phase and is increasingly used in interventions internationally. However, developing the knowledge and skills for collaborative analysis of data is generally not part of the teacher training college curricula (e.g. Gummer & Mandinach, 2015), and there is a general consensus that such PLD is needed (e.g. Schildkamp & Kuiper, 2010). This situation has led to the rise of in-service teacher PD on data use (e.g. Lai & Schildkamp, 2016), and thus, teacher PLD in this aspect is therefore critical if the LSM is to succeed. Similarly, in Chapter Four we outlined the knowledge and skills required by partners for effective enactment of the LSM, and these skills are generally not taught to teachers or researchers either (Snow, 2016). Thus PLD in general, and given our focus on improving teaching, teacher PLD more specifically, is vital if the LSM is to succeed in improving valued student outcomes.

We use the term 'professional learning and development' in preference to the more common 'professional development'. This is because, over time, the term professional development has become associated with delivery of information to teachers in order to change their practice. Professional development in our view has connotations of something that is 'done to' teachers. Including professional learning in the construct on the other hand emphasises that individuals create professional knowledge by interacting with information in ways that challenge previous understandings and create new meaning (Timperley, 2011). Professional learning implies much more active engagement by participants, not just attendance in workshops. Emphasising professional learning and not just professional development is more consistent with our view of teaching as requiring adaptive expertise, and teachers, leaders and schools as partners in a research-practice partnership, not merely as research subjects.

Another way we signal key underlying principles of our approach to PLD is in the way we often refer to the improvements we seek to make in teachers' knowledge and practice as 'fine-tuning' teacher instruction (e.g. Lai, McNaughton, Amituanai-Toloa, et al., 2009). We use the term 'fine-tune' to echo Wenger (1998) who writes that learning within a community of practice involves evolving forms of mutual engagement, understanding and tuning their enterprise and developing repertoires, styles and discourses. We also use it to recognise that the teachers we come to work with are already, on the whole, well-trained, qualified and capable professionals. Our evidence over years of applying the LSM is that, in general, from the outset of successive applications, the leaders and teachers already employed instructional and leadership practices generally consistent with those identified in the literature as 'best practice'. We have not needed, in most LSM applications, to bring overall patterns of teaching up to a base competence level; rather we have sought to fine-tune teaching to move it from effective to even more effective. Evidence for this base level of teacher competence is that the most common profile of student learning in the clusters of schools we have worked with is that students, on average, have achievement rates lower than students nationally but also already have progress parallel to national rates. These parallel rates of progress suggest that the schools serving lower socio-economic communities we work with are generally already as effective as other schools nationally but that this is not sufficient to close the achievement gaps (Lai, McNaughton, Amituanai-Toloa, et al., 2009). Given this pattern, we have not needed in general to design PLD that improves teaching in order that students progress at the same rate as other students but in order that groups already making parallel progress can make the accelerated progress needed to close achievement gaps. However, even when there is overall lower teacher capability, there is always variation in the system such that there are teachers who demonstrate effective practices that can be fine-tuned and spread to other teachers; or a series of effective practices across teachers that can be fine-tuned. In this way, as we argued in previous chapters, we have consistently found variability across the system that can be capitalised on and fine-tuned.

PLD as Resourcing: Key Principles

Thinking of the second phase as providing resources, and especially in the form of PLD, follows our concern to solve the five big challenges in educational change described in Chapter One. We have derived a set of principles for PLD as resourcing on the evidence that they are necessary to build the capability required in schools, and for the sustainability of the LSM.

Key Principle One: Profiling Before Resourcing

The most important underlying principle is that understanding student and teacher learning needs, with respect to an agreed valued learning outcome, always comes before designing a PLD plan. This is a key concept of the LSM

'Contextualising of effective practice to local contexts' and is enacted in the structure of the LSM, where Phase 1: Profiling is positioned before any resourcing. (See Chapter Two where we also we discussed the logic and research underpinning our approach, and also explained the rationale for this sequence, which is used in every LSM application.)

This principle is also consistent with the literature on PLD that is effective. A best evidence synthesis of teacher PLD that formed much of the basis of our original thinking into the LSM development (Timperley et al., 2007) identified that PLD approaches that develop teachers' knowledge without first establishing student and teacher learning needs were generally only effective under two circumstances. The first circumstance is when teachers begin with low levels of knowledge and skill in the target domain. In this circumstance, providing teachers with clear guidelines and specific teaching techniques can be helpful. The other circumstance is when the PLD content focus is very narrow. For example, efforts to develop geography teachers' teaching of map reading skills or primary teachers' development of some spelling strategies have made an impact on these narrow aspects of student learning, despite provision of only limited PLD opportunities. In such cases though, these improvements did not transfer from the narrow focus to the broader areas of geography or reading comprehension achievement (Timperley, 2011).

Neither of these special circumstances apply in the contexts within which we work. Firstly, as we discussed in more depth earlier, the teachers with whom we partner generally tend to have sound foundational knowledge of the aspects of learning and teaching we are seeking to change. Secondly, the kinds of valued learning outcomes addressed in LSM applications are broad and ambitious outcomes such as achieving equitable outcomes in high stakes national qualifications or in reading comprehension achievement; achieving gains in specific sub-aspects of these, such as map reading or spelling, is not enough of a goal given our commitment to addressing stubborn, longstanding issues of educational inequity. Achieving meaningful changes that make a real difference for learners is much more complex and requires more complex forms of PLD.

Our approach also addresses the longstanding criticisms of PLD as being decontextualised from teachers' contexts and their students (Darling-Hammond & Richardson, 2009; Guskey, 2003; Timperley et al., 2007). For example, Guskey's (2003) review of 13 lists of effective PLD showed that, despite the emphasis on student performance, less than half the lists mention the importance of using analyses of student learning data to guide PLD activities.

Key Principle Two: Engaging Teachers in PLD

The second principle is that the PLD has to engage teachers, regardless of its form. It is widely accepted that a great deal of teacher PLD fails to be engaging for teachers, or as one teacher eloquently said, 'I hope I die during an in-service session because the transition between life and death would be so subtle' (Sparks, 2004, p. 247). Learning and implementing new approaches of any kind for any one of any age is challenging and requires a high level of motivation to engage with the PD on the part of learners. Developing PLD that is engaging is vital if PLD is to be effective (Garet, Porter, Desimone, Birman, & Yoon, 2001; Hunzicker, 2011).

We assume that school leaders, typically principals, come to our sessions with some existing motivation and commitment to learn. This is firstly because these leaders are usually the ones who formed the original partnership with us as researchers to solve an agreed problem. This is also because participation in LSM applications is typically voluntary at the level of clusters of schools and individual schools. NZ has a self-governing school system (Chapter Two), and as such schools are not required to collaborate with neighbouring schools or, except in exceptional circumstances, to participate in particular PLD programmes or other interventions. Hence, any agreement to partner is indicative of their commitment to the joint work. However, because of the whole school focus, participation in PLD and other LSM activities is not voluntary for other leaders in the schools who are typically teacher leaders, or for teachers. Thus we cannot assume that teachers and other leaders come to PLD as willing and already enthusiastic, self-motivated participants. Any PLD needs to focus on engaging teachers and school leaders, with an emphasis on engaging teachers given our focus on improving teaching.

There are many ways to engage teachers in PLD in an LSM application, but two in particular is commonly used across all. First, we make the PLD relevant to teachers by developing the shared focus on an agreed problem of practice. This is a key emphasis of the DBR tradition that the LSM draws on where there is a focus on solving problems of practice (e.g. Anderson & Shattuck, 2012; Snow, 2015) and has also been emphasised in the literature on PLD (e.g. Darling-Hammond & Richardson, 2009). Timperley (2011), for example, points out that:

> unless there is a need to solve a specific problem of practice or to improve a particular outcome for students, there is little urgency or motivation to change and improve. (p. 47)

Second, we establish clear links between teaching and learning outcomes, as that is a key feature of PLD programmes that work (Timperley et al., 2007). Explicit links are made between the PLD in the Resourcing phase with the data and outcomes from the Profiling phase that preceded it. We foreground how the PLD content is relevant to the problem, the hypotheses and the co-designed solutions from the earlier phase. These explicit links also function to keep building the knowledge and skills across phases in a form of 'deliberate practice' (Ericsson & Pool, 2016), as well as inducting teachers who were not present earlier into the PLD.

An example of the linkages comes from the Profiling phase in an application with primary schools. During the profiling phase we hypothesised that one explanation for a plateau in the development of reading after Year Six was that students were not being extended into deeper aspects of reading such as synthesis, analysis and critical literacy as much as was optimal. We began each PLD session about extended discussion or critical literacy by re-presenting slides showing graphs of patterns of student achievement data and graphs of teaching patterns and discussing with participants the relationship we theorised between the two and why we predicted that changing the classroom pattern would change the student learning pattern.

Key Principle Three: Collaborative Analysis of Data Cycles, Not Silver Bullets

New approaches introduced in a PLD are not presented as 'silver bullets' assumed to be effective so long as they are enacted with integrity. Rather, they are presented as solutions hypothesised to make a difference for learners and which were generated and agreed to by the partnership as a whole. As such, it is vital that these hypotheses are trialled, monitored, tested, adapted or rejected in big and small cycles of collaborative analysis of data *as part of the PLD*. The rationales and supporting evidence for the importance of collaborative analysis of data have been elaborated in earlier chapters, in particular Chapter Two. They include, for example, and the need to understand and test possible solutions through contextualisation (e.g. Lai & McNaughton, 2009), recognising and enabling teachers as experts with complex sets of knowledge and skills (rather than as procedural technicians) (e.g. Darling-Hammond & Bransford, 2005; Hatano & Inagaki, 1986); and the need to build both self and collective efficacy of teachers through the co-design (e.g. Bandura, 1995).

Big cycles tend to be the formal, systematic cycles of collaborative analyses of data undertaken at the start and end of each phase to alter aspects of the LSM for the next phase; and small cycles are the cycles that happen (often more informally and sometimes ad hoc) within a phase. The purpose of these cycles is to make solutions more effective in terms of student outcomes. An example of a big cycle is when we designed PLD in Phase 2 to focus on effective vocabulary instruction because the collaborative analysis in Phase 1 suggested that this was an area of weakness. An example of a small cycle is when teachers acted on the results of the collaborative analysis in Phase 1 and altered their classroom practices *before* the PLD in Phase 2 commenced.

These big and small cycles take place at multiple levels. For example, they occur at the cluster level using data about broad patterns of teaching and student learning across all schools in the cluster; and at classroom level, using data about the patterns of an individual teacher and the students' learning in that class. We also promote the importance of individuals and groups of teachers engaging in teaching as small cycles at the micro-level, especially in teacher's own classrooms. Teachers are encouraged to collect data on the effectiveness of co-designed approaches to teaching they have learnt from the LSM PLD in order to refine the approach for their next lesson. The cycles are also of varying duration – longitudinally over the course of the whole LSM application which could be three years or longer, to annual analyses in phases; to small cycles that might not extend beyond investigating the effect of a new approach on student learning within a single lesson.

Cycles involving collaborative analysis of data are nested within other cycles. An individual teacher's analysis of data about the effectiveness of a classroom-based intervention designed on the basis of class-level evidence is nested within a team-level analysis (such as a year level or subject area team), which is nested within the school's analysis, which is nested in the cluster-level analysis led by the research team. Who conducts and discusses the analysis at these different levels therefore varies from individual teachers to teams to schools to clusters. Table 1 (Chapter Four) provides an example of the various across-school and within-school PLCs, and the kinds of data collaboratively discussed in each PLC for one LSM intervention.

Key Principle Four: The Social Construction of New Forms of Expertise

Previous chapters have addressed the central importance of PLCs to our work and have discussed how PLCs are the sites for enacting the collaborative analysis of data. Similarly, the PLD that is co-designed and delivered in the partnership also takes place within these PLCs. We have explained the logic for using PLCs with supporting evidence in previous chapters. Here we wish to point out that PLCs as effective sites for PLD are also implicated in the PLD literature (e.g. Lai & Schildkamp, 2016). For example, a literature review on PLD concluded that PLCs meet the criteria of effective PLD as it provides sustained, job-embedded, collaborative teacher learning strategies (Darling-Hammond & Richardson, 2009). In Chapter Four, there is an example structure of a PLC in a cluster of schools which gives some indication of the composition of and number of PLCs that involve PLD.

In previous chapters, we discussed how the LSM draws on concepts from socio-cultural theorising and socio-cognitive theorising (See Chapter Two). Professional learning is not simply the result of professional development activities led by PLD providers but arises from the community itself and the interactions within it. PLD in these communities therefore involves both direct forms of instruction, such as presentations of new content, and learning opportunities through social apprenticeship such as sense-making discussions with researchers and colleagues.

One LSM application, for example, involved a PLC comprised of researchers, teachers and literacy leaders who were tasked with driving the intervention in the school in 10 sessions across a year. These sessions involved direct instruction to build knowledge in particular areas of weakness identified from the profiling phase, an inquiry task using collaborative analysis of data based on the session focus which teachers had to develop and then carry out between sessions, followed by a critical discussion of the inquiry task in the next session. One session, for example, introduced theories and research relating the role of vocabulary in comprehension. The inquiry task for this session involved teachers designing a simple study carried out in the classroom which looked at building vocabulary through teaching. They then discussed the success and challenges of trying to do so in the following session.

Resourcing as Bespoke

The defining characteristic of resourcing is that it is a bespoke response to the strengths and needs identified in profile. It is bespoke both in terms of content (e.g. content-area focus) and process of delivery, including who actually delivers the PLD and what learning activities are provided. The focus of the resourcing is not and cannot be fully pre-determined because of the commitment to contextualising. In this way, the content of Phase 2: Resourcing is less defined than the content in Phase 1: Profiling. In the profiling phase, partners always develop knowledge about collecting, analysing and interpreting student, classroom and school (and beyond) data, and skills for discussing these data in PLCs. The specific instruments, analyses and forms of data representation can vary across applications but these elements are consistent across all. These data processes continue in Phase 2 and are in essence mandatory. But although there are broad principles applied in the resourcing phases of all LSM applications, the actual learning is less constrained than other phases.

Therefore, we do not have existing sets of resources or programmes of content that we roll out with only minor modifications. This does not mean that we ignore what we have learnt from previous applications. Rather, learning from successive LSM applications allows us to become more efficient and strengthens our ability to identify and test hypotheses in similar contexts. In such situations, we would suggest, on the basis of our previous research and experiences, a possible hypothesis that we consider worthy of testing. However, we still put that hypothesis on the table to be tested alongside other hypotheses.

Just as we do not employ pre-packaged existing sets of resources or programmes of content, we do not expect the PLD we develop to address problems in a specific context to be effective 'as is' in other contexts and be delivered in similar ways. Rather knowledge of previously effective modes of delivering PLD is brought to the table to be tested for appropriateness in the new context.

Our approach, however, does not reduce the important place in education for strong evidence-based programmes such as in literacy, Reading Recovery (Clay, 1993) or Reading Apprenticeship (Schoenbach, Greenleaf, & Murphy, 2012). Clearly, there are situations when such programmes would be appropriate and effective responses to identified needs in a particular context. However, as we argued in Chapter One, even strong evidence-based programmes show variation across contexts (Coalition for Evidence-Based Policy, 2013), and understanding and adapting a programme to local needs can add to a programme's success (Treviño et al., 2018), which brings us to the tensions inherent in our bespoke approach.

Tensions

A key tension is between efficiency (in terms of time and money to design a resource) and effectiveness (in terms of the impact on student outcomes). There are trade-offs to be made. An alternative and more efficient approach to resourcing would be to conduct the profiling, but then select a tested off-the-shelf programme that best fits the profile of need. This is the approach that the Centre for Data-Driven Reform in Education's data use PD programme takes. The primary purpose of analysing the data is to select an intervention from a series of approved interventions that have met their proposed criteria for having demonstrated success (Centre for Data-Driven Reform, 2011).

This approach could work well to solve problems which are clearly defined and less complex. However, even successful off-the-shelf packages might need to be adapted to fit the local contexts (e.g. Treviño et al., 2018). Moreover, bespoke models of resourcing are needed in instances of complex and longstanding issues, where multiple solutions have been applied in the past with little systematic success and where new approaches need to be adopted. The LSM attempts to navigate these tensions by drawing on such effective interventions, but then contextualising them in collaboration with partners to fit the local context and needs.

PLD Model: Cascading Structure

The model for PLD delivery is a cascade model because dissemination of PLD content is typically designed to flow from PLCs comprising school and across-school leaders and the research partners to school-based PLCs and into classrooms. We are aware though of the somewhat negative associations the term cascading has. In the literature, cascading is commonly used to refer to PLD where individual teachers attend off-site work training sessions and disseminate new learning back to colleagues in their own schools (Kennedy, 2005; Solomon & Tresman, 1999). The first limitation of many cascade models is related to the original PLD that teachers attend before disseminating. Often this is a training session where teachers attend alongside other teachers from a wide range of different schools. Such training sessions suffer the problem of being decontextualised from one's own setting (Darling-Hammond & Richardson, 2009; Kennedy, 2005). Moreover, training implies treating teachers as technicians who can be taught discrete skills rather than as adaptive experts developing broader and deeper understandings that they can tailor to their own classroom context.

Another drawback of cascade models in general is that what is disseminated is often procedure focussed and, even when the original PLD at the top of the cascade, is knowledge focussed, there can be too little attention paid to the underlying value and purpose of the content as it trickles down (Solomon & Tresman, 1999). Without an integrated theory, new content may be enacted in inconsistent ways (Timperley et al., 2007).

Mitigating the Risks

There are fundamental features of the LSM's conception of PLD that mitigate against these known drawbacks. Firstly, the PLD occurs in a partnership focussed on a pressing problem, with joint hypothesis testing and co-design of proposed solutions developed prior to the application of the cascade process. Thus, there is no one-off workshop decontextualised from a pressing problem and no solutions that have not been co-designed with representatives from schools. Secondly, in our model, 'dissemination' from cluster-level to school-level PLD contexts is led by leaders, not by classroom teachers as in the models critiqued by Solomon and Tresman (1999).

Thirdly, the model of dissemination is not a simple one-way transmission model from the person attending the one-off workshop teaching it to others. Rather, there are multiple inter-connected networks of PLCs with overlapping members focussed on sense-making around the PLD (Lai & McNaughton, 2018). In most applications, there are also leaders of the various PLCs tasked with ensuring that the PLD is enacted and coherent across the whole school and whole group of schools (Lai & McNaughton, 2018; see also Chapter Four which provides a table of the various PLCs and their composition). In this sense, dissemination takes on a very different meaning, one that is focussed on sense-making around the PLD and incorporates feedback loops across different PLCs designed to enact the PLD. Fourthly, these feedback loops serve as a form of integrity check on whether and how the PLD has been enacted at the different levels; with some of the integrity checks being formally undertaken by researchers (Lai et al., 2014) and taken on by school leaders post-intervention (Lai & McNaughton, 2018).

Over the applications of the LSM, we have employed additional strategies to support school leaders to contextualise PLD content from the cluster-level into school-based PLD opportunities. The most important of these utilises the concept of social apprenticeship (Wenger, 1998). Our approach is to promote the idea that school-level processes should mirror cluster-level processes. For example, researchers lead PLD in cluster-level PLCs in the same way we expect school leaders to lead PLD in school-level PLCs.

A useful metaphor for thinking about the relationship between the different levels of learning, between cluster (across-school) and within-school PLCs, and between different school PLCs, is the metaphor of fractals. In mathematics, a fractal is a geometric shape that can be split into parts, each of which is, approximately, a smaller copy of the whole. Fractals have a scaling shape; magnifying a small section of a fractal will reveal a pattern that is similar to the fractal as a whole and to other small sections. The idea that sections of fractal patterns have self-similarity (i.e. the parts look like the whole) mirrors the process of PLD at different levels of LSM clusters. An important reason we are drawn to fractals as a metaphor for PLD is that shared design properties do not imply homogeneity (Eglash, 1999) but, rather, spontaneity within a general design structure. Learning opportunities for cluster leaders are not exactly the same as those for teachers in schools or for students in classrooms, but there are underlying similarities. For example, in our cluster-level collaborative analysis of data sessions, and in PLD opportunities attended by leaders, the patterns of teaching and learning identified in the analyses of data, and the implications for teacher learning are both investigated at the level of the cluster, that is at the level of the aggregate of all schools in the cluster. School leaders are provided with analyses of data at the level of their own school, and during and after the cluster-level data discussions they are expected to consider the patterns for their own school and how these patterns are similar or different to the patterns for the cluster as a whole. Similar analyses might also be provided at the classroom level. Similarly, they also participate in PLD opportunities at the cluster level that they are expected to tailor to fit best with their own school's learning and teaching profile. In this way, the fractal (Cluster) is reflected in the smaller version of the fractal (school or classroom), and in each fractal there are commonalities, but not homogeneity.

A risk in the cascading by leaders is that the PLD content and the learning and teaching data that gave rise to that PLD content become uncoupled from one another. In such a case, the risk is that teachers in schools could be provided with PLD opportunities without knowing the student and teacher data that informed the design of PLD in the first place, particularly if some teachers had not participated in the profiling phase or have forgotten about the discussions there. As discussed earlier, this would remove a potentially powerful catalyst for teachers to engage in the PLD and could make opaque the theory of action sitting behind the PLD. To mitigate this risk, we have used various methods such as providing a short background prior to the PLD that explained the need for the PLD based on the local evidence, and a brief summary of the hypothesis testing and co-designed solutions that led to the PLD.

A second risk is if our profiling of schools' PLD capability or if schools themselves indicate that leaders need support in disseminating and contextualising the PLD in their schools. To mitigate this risk, we add additional PLD and resources to support leaders disseminate and contextualise the PLD. For example, in one application of the LSM, a series of presentations and other resources was developed to support school and literacy leaders lead PLD about disciplinary literacy in their own schools. One such resource was a presentation on how to use and interpret reports from the asTTle reading achievement tool (Hattie et al., 2005) that was used in the cluster. This was because literacy leaders reported in the profiling phase that while most teachers knew the achievement levels of students in reading, they were not using the formative aspects of the tool to identify and address more specific aspects of reading development. All presentations included detailed facilitation notes and some also included an audio commentary that the researcher recorded. Leaders chose whether to follow the provided materials quite closely or to use these as springboards for their own presentations, and how they finally implemented these sessions was checked against teacher reports and self-reports as part of the wider LSM intervention.

In several applications we have also designed and delivered PLD about PLD, that is, we have supported leaders or facilitators provide PLD to teachers. In another application of the LSM across countries, there were sessions where in-country facilitators from universities and ministries reflected on effective PLD they had experienced themselves, learnt about features of PLD identified as effective in the literature (e.g. Timperley et al., 2007) and began to design PLD opportunities consistent with the literature for teachers in their own context.

The Role of School Leaders

Implicit in the cascade model we have described is the important role of school leaders that includes both leaders holding formal positions (e.g. principals) and those tasked with leadership. Our model demands that leaders do much more than 'outsource' PLD to other providers. While leaders are not necessarily the key people responsible for developing new learning in the school, they are required to take an active leadership role in the resourcing phase. Previously, we discussed how we view teaching as requiring adaptive expertise. We regard leadership as requiring adaptive expertise too. School-based leaders need to think strategically about the similarities and differences of the cluster-level versus school-level profiles of teaching and learning, and the resourcing implications of those profiles. Just as the resourcing provided in LSM differs from application to application, resourcing must also be adapted to individual schools. No school will ever have exactly the same profile as another school within the same cluster, let alone the same profile as the aggregated cluster-level profile. Because of this, the PLD resources and materials we provide leaders are not in the form of scripted workshops they or anyone else can simply deliver verbatim within their own schools. Leaders need to ensure that PLD designed and provided at the cluster level is tailored to the school level. Teachers then, of course, have to ensure in turn that PLD designed and provided at the school level is tailored to best meet the specific profile of their own classroom context. This expectation of leaders is consistent with a seminal meta-analysis that identified five aspects of leadership associated with higher than expected student achievement (Robinson et al., 2008). The fifth dimension of leadership of promoting and participating in teacher learning and development had twice the effect size of the other four aspects of school leadership, and in essence, this is what we have tasked school leaders in the LSM to do.

Issues with the Cascade

The LSM has not overcome all the inherent limitations of cascading structures. In one literacy intervention, the evidence suggested that only some of the professional learning survived the transfer from the research/school leader PLCs into school-based PLCs into classrooms. Our evidence suggested that the PLD was associated with positive shifts in some of the aspects of literacy teaching that have been promoted as responses to the profiling needs, but not all. The general pattern was that easier-to-shift aspects such as increasing the amount of time students spent reading content-area texts improved but harder-to-shift aspects such as more dialogicity and criticality did not. This instructional risk has been found in other large-scale interventions in both literacy and science where challenging and complex changes to existing PCK and practices are required (McNaughton, 2018). This particular pattern is consistent also with the extant literature. Internationally, previous studies have found, for example, that teachers find it very difficult to change classroom discourse patterns, even when they want to (Alozie, Moje, & Krajcik, 2010; Groenke, 2010).

We hypothesise that these areas of limited shifts are related to weaknesses in the PLD provided at the top of the cascade. The PLD did not provide sufficient, varied opportunities over an extended-enough period of time to develop leaders' knowledge of the more complex aspects of disciplinary literacy teaching. Also, the cascade itself was weak in that the PLD about deeper features of literacy became progressively diluted as it flowed to the school level. In general, however, the cascade model has worked well, particularly in less complex school structures such as primary schools, which are generally not organised into semi-autonomous departments.

Other Forms of Resourcing

As discussed, PLD has been the most important but not the only action taken in the partnerships to address the problems profiled in the first phase of LSM. Here, we briefly consider other forms of resourcing employed in our model.

A resourcing focus in addition to PLD is illustrated by an application of the LSM that operated across 43 primary schools within three countries over three years. The overarching goal was to improve literacy outcomes for primary school students through key deliverables, including intensive PLD for principals, teachers, and leaders of literacy to enhance understandings about the nature of students' literacy learning, leadership and management for change, and the development of context-specific literacy resources. Two resources in particular are the focus here: assessment tool development and book development (wordless books and big books on non-fiction texts).

The profiling phase revealed that the assessment tools in literacy that would provide the information required for profiling of the sort used in the LSM did not currently exist in these countries. This led to the co-construction of formative literacy assessment tools. In accordance with the DBR approach, these tools were co-designed with in-country specialists, aligned to the curriculum and each country's context and focus area, informative about student's strengths and areas of need, and reliable and replicable.

A second key resource activity during Phase 2 was the co-construction of a series of books for use across countries, and a series of books in languages specific to each country. The first set of books to be developed was wordless books. Wordless books are picture books without words and no set narrative, although there is still storyline. It is used to develop children's confidence in reading, encourages the use of contextual cues and encourages retelling, among other literacy advantages. Wordless books (based on existing NZ Ministry of Education publications) were a quick, low-cost means to provide new resources that targeted student learning challenges identified in the profiling phase. (In all three countries, a key contributor to literacy success was hypothesised as students' ability to generate language and to compose stories with meaning.) The wordless books supported this focus and responded well to the multi-lingual contexts of each country. The themes of these books were co-developed in each country, and the contents were specific to each context.

The book development process varied across countries. Publishing companies were engaged to support the development process, working in collaboration with the research and development team, and with in-country language experts. It required a balance between demands of getting the texts into classrooms as quickly as possible with the importance of engaging local authors and illustrators, and involving in-country partners in all stages of development. The involvement of language experts was particularly important. Ensuring each

Ministry of Education are the copyright holders for the books was important for sustainability.

The second sets of books to be developed were big books for shared reading which focussed on non-fiction texts; again these were in response to gaps found in all three countries during the profiling phase. Big books are large-sized books that a teacher can use when reading with a group of students. Shared reading was a valued teaching approach in each country; however, there were few big books to support it. The addition of non-fiction texts to the suite of existing fiction readers was intended to support vocabulary development and concept development in a way that aligned with each country's curriculum.

Contextualising narratives and illustrations to each country has contributed to high engagement with the books by students and teachers. In one Pacific nation, three titles integrated a local *kastom stori* with its associated scientific concepts. This was an innovative approach designed to uphold indigenous knowledge, while also introducing scientific concepts and vocabulary. In another, the development of dual language readers was a further innovation, designed to support schools with the identified challenge of the introduction of English in Year Four while continuing to advance the native language. In the final nation, a priority concern was to promote the native language. Existing native language resources were limited and plain in comparison to the English language resources. High-quality illustrations and production, and dialect translations were important for enhancing student engagement in learning the native language.

These new resources were introduced with accompanying PLD. While teacher notes accompanying the books were valued, face-to-face PLD was essential for building teachers' confidence to use new books. The introduction of the new books was an integrated component of the overall PLD strategy and provided a tangible mechanism for teachers to apply the strategies learnt through PLD. Both PLD and teacher notes were targeted to areas of student need and provided strategies that teachers could employ with a range of published and school-made resources. The co-constructed wordless and worded books were mobilised across all schools within each country, alongside PLD facilitated by in-country literacy specialists, focussing on effective use of these books for different learners.

Chapter Six

Sustainability of the LSM

Conceptions of sustainability differ. Sustainability can be conceived as an outcome. For example, a literacy intervention is sustained when literacy achievement levels continue to improve after the end of the intervention. It can also be conceived as a process, for example, the literacy intervention is sustained when schools continue using the literacy strategies they used during the intervention. In a process view, sustainability continues or maintains activities designed to improve school practices and teaching activities after the end of an intervention (Datnow, 2005). However, this idea assumes we know when the appropriate time has been reached to stop, and we are able to engage in the intervention until that point is reached. In the context of long-term research-practice partnerships with an intervention focus like the LSM, the assumption that there is a definite end to an intervention is problematic, and we discuss this later in this chapter. The process view also+ assumes that we know all there is to know about being effective through the intervention actions, activities or teaching practices and how they relate to outcomes of interest (Borman, 2005).

There is a further problem. The standard approach to interventions and their sustainability has been to assume that the intervention activities are still applicable after the intervention. This is without regard to the churn that is typical of the open complex systems of schools, namely changes in student demographics, changes in teachers and leaders, and systemic changes such as new curricula or new technologies. Such churn may necessitate different activities from those applied in an intervention. This does not mean that maintaining intervention activities in itself is unimportant; rather the activities need to be continually evaluated for their relevance to the changing features of the context and to the original goals of the intervention. This is fundamental to an iterative design process, continually evaluating the applicability of the intervention activities in light of the impact on the goals of the intervention (typically defined as improved valued student outcomes), and in light of the changing school environment which may necessitate an adaption of the existing activities to meet new needs, or even new activities.

Our conception of sustainability follows the principles and tenets of DBR, which is the main theoretical and methodological foundation of the LSM. These

Research-practice Partnerships for School Improvement:
The Learning Schools Model, 87–97
Copyright © 2020 by Mei Kuin Lai, Stuart McNaughton, Rebecca Jesson and Aaron Wilson
Published under exclusive license
doi:10.1108/978-1-78973-571-020201007

principles foreground the importance of analysis of data for intervention design and redesign, and intervention effectiveness. So, rather than focus on maintaining an intervention, our view is that it is better to think of sustainability as a process of continued improvement to achieve valued student outcomes based on the intervention goals, content and activities. That is, maintenance involves school leaders and teachers continuing to improve their practices to achieve valuable student outcomes using the knowledge, skills and activities learnt in the intervention, and continually evaluating the applicability of these using cycles of collaborative analysis of data. These cycles of collaborative analysis of data can be seen as a form of ongoing evaluation. As such, a key goal of sustainability in the LSM is to develop an evaluative capability in schools.

Therefore in every application of the LSM there is a focus on developing the capability of school leaders and teachers to collaboratively analyse data as part of developing their capability to continue checking and adapting the applicability of the LSM activities and associated resources to their contexts and goals. Second, that there is a corresponding focus on handing over the responsibility of the collaborative analysis process so that this process is led by the school leaders and teachers.

While the focus on sustainability is the same, the activities and resources for sustainability vary across LSM applications, depending on whether the partnership is long term and on what constitutes the ongoing needs identified through the collaborative analysis. In one application, the focus for researchers collaborating with a group of leaders from across schools to analyse and use data to improve school practices was on how to hand over the collection of data to them, such that schools no longer relied on the researchers to collect and collate across-school data. In another, there was a greater focus on developing leadership capability to induct new teachers into the collaborative analysis process and the knowledge of the teaching practices designed through the LSM, and to attract new teachers to the schools based on the emerging data on teacher attrition.

Why Is Sustainability so Important for the LSM?

Research evidence is consistent in that changing schools in a sustainable way is a difficult process (e.g. Cuban, 2003; Timperley et al., 2007). Sustainability of ongoing improvements is fragile at best (Datnow, Borman, Stringfield, Overman, & Castellano, 2003). The problem is particularly pressing for reforms and interventions in schools serving culturally and linguistically diverse students, where there have been persistent achievement problems and longstanding difficulties in creating reforms that work to promote valued outcomes for these students. Schools that successfully implement reforms and improve achievement find it difficult to sustain them in the face of competing priorities, changing demands, changing student demographics and teacher and administrator turnover (Coburn, 2003; Datnow, 2005). Not surprisingly, there are very few studies that can demonstrate improvements in achievement after the end of a reform or an intervention. In their best evidence synthesis, Timperley et al. (2007) located only seven studies that could demonstrate sustained student outcomes following professional development interventions. Although each of these studies was associated with ongoing collaborative analysis of data and knowledge building processes similar to the collaborative analysis of data processes described in this book, sustainability was typically an additional rather than a central focus.

Many of the LSM applications have had an intervention focus with a general aim of addressing the longstanding issues of educational disparities for indigenous and ethnic minority students where there has been limited success at scale. The need for interventions that can continue to make achievement gains after their 'official end' is heightened in this context, particularly as these schools face significant challenges that impact on sustaining achievement outcomes, such as high teacher attrition. For example, in one application, two years after the end of Phase 3, we estimated that only about a third of teachers had taught a class for a full academic year the year before (Lai, McNaughton, Timperley et al., 2009). The context in which the LSM operates thus requires deliberate attention to induction and retention as goals for sustainability, and as such, this focus is built into the design of the LSM from the start through the collaborative analysis of data processes.

Designing for Sustainability: How Sustainability Is Developed Through the LSM

Sustainability is planned for through the overall application of the LSM, as we do not assume sustainability can and will occur independently or 'organically'. There are two ways we have built sustainability. Firstly, in every phase the partnership focuses on collaborative analysis of data. This is the component 'A', of the A, A+B, A+B+C design of the LSM (Chapter One). School leaders and teachers engage in collaborative analysis at least twice a year with researchers and more frequently with each other during the year in within-school and across-school PLCs (see Chapter Four). So, the first approach involves developing the capability of school leaders and teachers and other relevant partners in collaborative analysis of data, and to embed collaboratively analysis into schools' 'business as usual'. (The collaborative analysis process and its importance are described in previous chapters.)

The second approach is to have the final phase specifically dedicated to building sustainability (Phase 3). This phase continues the collaborative analysis of data and problem solving from prior phases and the resourcing for solutions, but adds deliberate analysis and planning for sustainability. That is why, in design terms, Phase 3 is considered an A, A+B, A+B+C design, as the collaborative analysis of data and resourcing continues but a focus on sustainability is added.

Sustainability in Phase 3

Phase 3 continues embedding the processes and implements specific practices to support sustainability. This takes several forms but is based on engaging in practices indicated through the analyses that will capitalise on and further develop the expertise in collaboratively collecting and analysing data. To this end, we have used practices such as school-initiated case studies of effective teachers, and teacher-led inquiry projects using collaborative analysis of data principles. The latter focuses on solutions within classrooms, and where results and reflections are shared across multiple schools in mini conferences or professional learning networks. (An example is described in Chapter Two.)

In some applications, specific PLD to develop leaders' knowledge and skills has been added to the modelling and incidental learning which occur through engaging in the processes. An example is the use of 'inquiry projects' with leaders as a PLD tool. Researchers worked with a group of about 25 teacher leaders from 12 different schools. Each session with these leaders consisted of a presentation of ideas and theory about a particular stage in a data analysis process, opportunities to plan with others how to apply this learning in their own project, discussion about their ongoing effectiveness of actions taken as a result of the data analysis, and so on. The content covered over the course of the year supported teachers to collaboratively analyse data on a specific issue of student learning in their class. The template for their final report that follows also gives an indication of the content covered in these PLD sessions (Fig. 3).

A key purpose of each of the deliberate practices described previously is to increase the number of teachers capable of collaborative analysis, which is all the more important to undertake in the final phase given the high teacher turnover rates described previously.

In other applications, we have added a focus on developing additional forms of resourcing for sustainability. The specific forms and focus of such resourcing are based on needs identified in the data and are always co-designed with the partners. One key area that required additional resourcing was the recruitment and induction of new staff. We described earlier how we developed specific inductions into the focus and patterns of teaching and professional learning in the schools to respond to the high rates of turnover. It is worth noting that like any problem to be solved, gathering data on the reasons for turnover was important to the partnership's response. We found that teacher turnover was not necessarily a negative indicator. In many cases it was a by-product of the success of the interventions. Schools reported that many of their staff obtained positions in other schools that were promotions. Resourcing to address this need firstly involved developing artefacts for attracting and recruiting new staff. These were in the form of advertisements for new positions that deliberately described the schools' engagement with the LSM, including a description of the nature of the LSM processes now 'owned' by the schools. One cluster of schools also worked closely with a local university to attract new graduates to their schools.

Developing resourcing for induction involved developing induction procedures, for example, procedures and related documents that would support teachers new to the school understand the processes and practices developed through the LSM. This was coupled with building systems and processes within the school to sustain the processes and practices developed through the LSM, such that these became schools' core business. For example, a key approach was to write into the school policies and assessment calendar details of the collaborative analysis of data cycles. The assessment calendar then provided a timetable of what

---

Leading Inquiries: Reporting Template

Profiling

A. Developing a profile of students' strengths and needs.

1. Summarise the problem of student learning you focussed on in this inquiry.
2. Describe how and why you first selected this problem of student learning at the beginning of your inquiry.
3. Describe the tools/measures/approaches you used to get a more detailed and accurate profile of students' learning in relation to that problem. Justify why you chose these approaches and tools.
4. Summarise your key findings about the nature and extent of the student problem, i.e., present your baseline student data and evidence.

B. Developing a profile of teaching strengths and needs.

5. Describe the main hypotheses you developed about factors that might contribute to this problem of student learning (e.g. particular features of teaching or out of school practices that were not as effective as they might be).
6. Explain why you hypothesised that these factors would contribute to the student learning problem. Give reasons and refer to professional readings, colleagues and experts you consulted, etc.
7. Explain how you tested your hypotheses about factors that might contribute to the problem of student learning, e.g., observations of teaching, student voice about out of school practices.
8. Summarise your key findings about possible causes of the problem of student learning identified in the profiling phase ,i.e., present your baseline data and evidence about teaching and other factors that affect student learning.

Intervention

1. Describe in detail the intervention you designed to address the student learning problem, i.e., exactly what did you plan to change? Be specific about actions, timelines, etc.
2. Explain in detail your theories about why that intervention would positively impact on the problem of student learning (i.e. explain the causal chain you theorised).
3. Describe in detail the sources of information you drew on to design your intervention (e.g. readings, courses, people).
4. Give specific examples of how you monitored the effectiveness of your intervention and made adaptations as you went along.

Fig. 3.　Reporting Template for Inquiry Projects.

Evaluation

1. Summarise evidence about key changes in teaching and other factors that influence student learning.
2. Summarise evidence about key shifts in the problem of student learning.
3. Write an overall evaluation of your intervention in terms of the causal chain you had theorised, i.e., to what extent was the intervention successful in changing factors such as teaching? To what extent were those changes in teaching effective in changing patterns of student learning?
4. Write a reflection on your own professional learning through this inquiry cycle.

Fig. 3. (*Continued*)

assessments were to be undertaken as a whole school and in many cases when the data were to be discussed and by which PLCs. All these resourcing actions meant that the school were not reliant on the institutional knowledge of key individuals who might leave the school, or on the incidental picking up of 'how we do things' at the school.

What We Have Learnt from Sustainability Studies

We have researched our claims about sustainability. We followed up schools two years immediately after the end of the third phase in three applications of the LSM. These three applications were interventions to improve literacy achievement. We collected achievement data two years after the third phase, and surveyed teachers. We examined sustainability in greater depth in two applications, where we also surveyed and interviewed leaders about their practices, analysed key documents (e.g. the school assessment calendar), carried out additional teacher surveys on their perspectives of leaders and conducted observations of a sample of PLCs. All of these measures were used to develop a theory of action about sustainability including the barriers to and enablers of sustainability. The results have been previously published and discussed (e.g. Lai, 2019; Lai & McNaughton, 2018; Lai et al., 2009, 2011), so in this section, we summarise the key outcomes across studies, before discussing the general principles of sustainability from these detailed studies and our other work.

Key Outcomes

Achievement in the two years after the interventions was examined by researchers via the statistical method of hierarchical linear modelling, through which we compared the rate of gain during and after the intervention. Achievement over the schools, on average, continued to improve at the rate it did during the intervention, namely between three to four months of progress in reading comprehension in addition to expected yearly progress (Lai et al., 2011). This is a substantial accomplishment given the paucity of research evidence for sustained improvements in achievement (Timperley et al., 2007) and is significant given the historical difficulties of raising achievement of culturally and linguistically diverse students in low socio-economic communities.

However, despite these gains, the modelling indicated that the gains were insufficient to reach parity with national distributions and national averages, and there were differences over summer and for students with different starting achievement levels. The data suggested several issues affecting parity: achievement issues in earlier year levels (thus necessitating an early intervention alongside one at the middle school years); the low achievement of absent students, and also transient students entering the school; and large drops in achievement in over the summer holidays in between academic years. There were also significant differences between schools, in that some schools made more gain than others.

School Practices

As we had predicted we found that the main school-based practice associated with sustainability was collaborative analysis of data both within a school and across schools. All schools continued to focus on improving reading comprehension and used the collaborative analysis of data cycles established during the LSM. These cycles were in the school assessment calendars and were considered part of the 'normal' school activities and processes. Within a school, PLCs at the syndicate (teachers teaching the same year levels), whole school and leadership levels enacted cycles of collaborative analysis of data in the year. This is where they collected student achievement information relating to their focus on improving achievement in reading comprehension, designed practices to address the needs identified, evaluated the impact of their practices on student achievement and then modified their practices in light of the evaluation data. All schools embedded the collaborative analysis of data processes into their normal school routines as part of a coherent school-wide programme. A focus on coherence included deliberate strategies to minimise involvement in school or outside activities that would detract from their focus on reading comprehension.

Across schools, similar collaborative analysis of data cycles were established albeit the focus was on the patterns across schools. Leaders or representatives from each school met regularly to examine the data across all schools in the cluster, and researchers were invited into those meetings. In this way, school leaders were inter-dependent with other educators in their cluster, and supported by research expertise. Moreover, school leaders led these collaborative inquiries and/or participated in both within-school and across-school communities. Leaders also provided funding and resources such as teacher release time to participate.

While the practices for sustainability were virtually identical across schools, there were fine-grained variations in how these practices were enacted that appeared to be associated with variations in school gains (Lai, McNaughton, Timperley et al., 2009). An analysis of the highest and lowest gain school in one application of the LSM suggested that the gains were related to two subtle differences. Firstly, the problems that the teachers in the higher gain school were trying to solve were framed very specifically. For example, they were trying to solve the drop in achievement between academic years based on the analysis of school data, which showed large drops in achievement between academic years. The problems that the teachers in the lower gain school were trying to solve were framed generically, for example, what was working well in the school reading programme. The second subtle difference between the higher and lower gain schools was how issues that impacted on valued student outcomes were framed. Specifically, were the issues that schools encountered treated as explanations for why teachers could not be more effective, or were they treated as problems to be solved? The higher gain school, for example, treated teacher turnover as a problem to be solved through induction and retention, while the lower gain school treated teacher turnover as an explanation for their achievement results. There is further evidence that these two subtle differences were related to achievement outcomes. When the lower gain school began to change their practices to more closely resemble the higher gain school, they made larger gains in achievement, in the order of about five months in addition to expected progress.

School Leaders' Beliefs and Supporting Structures

School leaders believed in the importance of analysing and using data collaboratively to sustain student achievement and believed that a key goal of sustainability was the improvement of student achievement. They further believed that the key levers to improving achievement were collaborative analysis of data, effective teaching based on that analysis, and partnerships with other schools and external agents including researchers. There was little variation in these core beliefs, which echoed the key tenets of the LSM. The similarity in leaders' beliefs to each other and with the LSM is not unexpected given that school leaders were part of the LSM design and redesign over three years. This provides further evidence that involving school leaders in designing an intervention supports their understanding of it.

What enabled school leaders to act on their beliefs was firstly a PLC structure created prior to the LSM intervention but refined during it, that was designed to function as part of school's core business. As mentioned in previous chapters, there were existing PLC structures which were co-opted for use in most LSM applications, such as the use of existing within-school PLCs as sites for collaborative analysis (Chapter Four). Secondly, there was on-going support from external experts (time and expertise) as partners in the collaboration. These experts were from other schools in the across-school PLCs and researchers from the original LSM application as part of their commitment to the partnership. The wider NZ policy approach, which we will discuss in the following section, also supported school leaders' approaches to sustainability.

School leader' theories of actions therefore comprised of a set of beliefs which supported sustainability, and supporting structures and resources and policy conditions that enabled them to act on their beliefs (Lai, 2019).

Conditions for Sustainability

From these studies, we identified a number of conditions for sustainability.

Collaborative Analysis of Data Involving External Expertise. Firstly, collaborative analysis of data involving external expertise be it from other schools or researchers appears to be important in sustaining achievement outcomes. The collaborative analysis of data processes has many features consistent with the literature on effective PLCs and networks (e.g. see the list of effective PLC characteristics identified by Bolam et al., 2005), and with empirical studies where PLCs have been associated with improvements in achievement (e.g. Lai & Schildkamp, 2016). Similar approaches to analysing and using data have also been associated with improvements in achievement in other interventions (e.g. Carlson et al., 2011). A recent meta-analyses on cost-benefit per participant for teacher PLD using similar analysis of data principles estimated a 98% chance that such PLD will produce benefits that exceed the cost. They further estimated a total benefit (categorised as taxpayers, participants, others and indirect benefits) of $13,493 against the net programme cost of $110 per participant.

Before our own follow-up studies, our evidence for the significance of collaborative analysis of data was largely by association. By this we mean, collaborative analysis of data was part of the LSM and associated with achievement gains. Even given what we have found in the follow-up studies, and given the mounting evidence, there remains the need to formally test the claim for the impact of collaborative analysis of data on student outcomes.

The Important Role of School Leaders. As per previous chapters, our evidence implicates yet again the role of schools leaders. In this case, their role in enacting collaborative analysis of data, with leaders demonstrating leadership characteristics and practices identified as effective (e.g. Bolam et al., 2005; Fulton, Doerr, & Britton, 2010; Peurach, 2016). These characteristics and practices are also consistent with dimensions of effective leadership identified in a seminal meta-analysis (Robinson et al., 2008). For example, school leaders led at least one school PLC and participated in both across-school and within-school PLCs. This, as we have indicated before, reflects the dimension of leadership with the highest impact on student achievement identified in Robinson's et al. meta-analysis, the dimension of participating and leading teacher learning and development.

Planning for Sustainability. The findings support our idea that interventions more generally and specifically, in this case, the LSM, need to be deliberately planned to be sustainable. By this we mean, the processes for and structures to enable sustainability need to be designed during the intervention, and we do not assume sustainability can and will occur independently.

Alignment with National Policy. Competition from other priorities including policy priorities has been identified as a barrier to sustainability (Datnow, 2005). Thus, it is worth noting that the key school practices for sustainability are consistent with the wider NZ national educational policy environment, and this coherence could have also contributed to the sustainability of the LSM. For example, the NZ curriculum focuses on teaching as inquiry (see Chapter Two), and a recent NZ Ministry of Education initiative was launched to develop PLCs across schools focussed on collaborative analysis of data (Ministry of Education, n.d.-d). Moreover, the NZ educational system does not have high stakes accountability and national testing, although it has national tests later in schooling and has national and/or regional accountability systems (Lai & Schildkamp, 2016). Under these conditions, schools may be more willing to share information about practices and students, and collaborative analysis of data can thrive.

Issues

At the start of this chapter, we indicated that our definition of sustainability becomes difficult with partnerships that endure over some time, and where there may be no definite end. In such instances, the researchers and schools continue to collaborate, for example, to address new problems of practice that have emerged from the original collaboration, such as a focus on writing following the end of an application of the LSM focussed on reading. Enduring has also come to mean periods when researchers are not actively engaged with a group of schools, but subsequently return to work more actively again with those schools as needed.

This adds to complexity of terminology, in this case the notion of 'enduring'. We have experienced this when several years after a series of LSM applications concluded, schools chose to partner with us again, albeit for new foci and with new goals. For example, three clusters of schools were involved in a national evaluation project which was still a partnership between the researchers who were now part of a wider project team and the schools. These new partnerships focussed on building evaluative capability which extended the collaborative analysis of data principles developed in the LSM, and focussed on the same and additional curriculum areas. These new partnerships can be viewed as new applications of the LSM; but they can also be viewed as a form of sustainability of the original application, given the similarities between the partners and the new partnership focus and given that the new applications leveraged off and continued with the capability that had already been built.

If we consider sustainability as ended according to the evaluation periods and the specified time over which an intervention has been implemented, then sustainability has a definite start and end point. Similarly, if we only consider sustainability in terms of funding for a particular project or tasks, then sustainability also has a definite start and end. In this view, even our most enduring partnership can be viewed as a series of discrete but inter-related LSM applications. However, if we consider sustainability as the design-based learning through collaborative partnerships, then collaborations do endure as new funding has been obtained and the learning using aspects of the LSM has informed subsequent applications. This latter view positions learning as continuing across multiple applications in the same partnership even though the learning might lead to a new curriculum area or focus of the partnership.

Another issue we faced when defining sustainability is around the notion of sustainability of the process and sustainability of the content. For example, we could view the LSM focus on sustainability as process focussed, as ongoing collaborative analysis of data is foregrounded and knowledge of the content-area (in most cases literacy) is placed more in the background. However, we could also view collaborative analysis of data as a form of 'content' in the same way as data literacy could be conceived of as content. This issue of whether collaborative analysis of data is positioned as process or content is not just an issue for the LSM, but for all interventions with similar inquiry and data-use focus, and where solutions for sustainability are needed.

Chapter Seven

Learning to Learn

A bold claim has been made that under appropriate conditions practice-embedded research approaches like DBR can have two functions. One is to solve the local problem or challenge. The second is that in so doing, they can also contribute to our understanding of education. The latter is a claim that we can generate knowledge that adds to the wealth of evidence-based knowledge, contributing to educational sciences.

Our claim is that an approach like the LSM can make this contribution to both methodological and conceptual understandings. Moreover, the conceptual understandings can be at all levels of educational systems: that of the micro-system of the teacher and students and processes of teaching and learning; at the level of the school and its organisational properties; school and community relationships; pathways within- and across-schools and post-school; as well as the understanding of larger aggregates of systems, such as districts. In principle it can be about resources conceived very broadly, from micro-properties of pedagogy through relationships among and between families and schools through to system infrastructure.

The good news is that we have growing evidence for these claims over time and contexts through the 15+ years of research into the LSM. In this chapter we provide examples of some of these contributions, and we explain how we, as researchers in the partnerships, have learned more. But more importantly we provide explanations for the conditions under which this knowledge is more or less likely, essentially identifying the enablers and constraints for knowledge building in practice-embedded research approaches like DBR. Given we claim that applications of the LSM have a knowledge-building function, we end the chapters with thoughts on what we still need to learn.

Contributing to Methodology

We have had to be agile and inventive in our methods. One example of this occurs as we come to select appropriate measures. It is a tenet of our discipline in social sciences that where possible one uses tried and true measures so that we can add to the cumulative knowledge by making comparisons and contrasts with other

Research-practice Partnerships for School Improvement:
The Learning Schools Model, 99–115
Copyright © 2020 by Mei Kuin Lai, Stuart McNaughton, Rebecca Jesson and Aaron Wilson
Published under exclusive license
doi:10.1108/978-1-78973-571-020201008

research using the common measures. And this can be met in the LSM applications often when the objective is achievement and where judgements are based on national standardised indicators of progress and level.

But a core assumption is that problems are a product of and constitute the local context. We have discussed this concept of context in Chapter Two. What this means is that in the process of trying to understand the local challenge, measures need to be developed that can capture the features and nuances of the possible explanations for that challenge, and also can provide metrics for the adequacy of the solutions. This is discussed in depth by Bryk et al. (2015). It is the need to be able to develop fit for purpose assessments or measures which nevertheless deliver believable and robust measures.

But this is in essence what good research should be like, whatever the approach. Adopting fit for purpose measures to suit the question and the context. In this section, however, we want to explain how we came to learn about what an appropriate research design would look like, and how we have needed to learn how to make that design work. The tension we came to understand was between needing to be flexible and to be able to iteratively modify foci, and yet retain a defensible research design, one that can meet criteria for robustness. In what follows, we outline the challenges for robustness that the LSM faces, and then how we learned what a workable and defensible methodological solution might look like.

Learning about 'What Works, for Whom, under What Conditions and at Scale'

'What works' statements through Clearing Houses and research syntheses (e.g. the Institute of Education Sciences What Works Clearinghouse https://ies.ed.gov/ncee/wwc/) have become the stock in trade of educational sciences. And we take seriously the need to rigorously establish what worked in solving a local challenge. But Bryk et al. (2015) have criticised this push to focus only on 'what works' for reasons we also have learned to acknowledge. They argue that the inherent variability in educational change and the complex and open nature of educational systems, means that the question 'Improvement Science' approaches need to answer (which is similar to questions that practice-embedded research approaches like DBR need to answer), is what worked for whom under what conditions and at scale.

In DBR-type approaches like the LSM, there is the added concern. That is to be able to learn from the evidence to identify possible solutions to on-the-ground challenges, and then to co-design, test and redesign for increasingly more effective solutions, learning through each iteration. A fixed inflexible design does not allow that.

RCTs as the Gold Standard?   Both 'What works' summaries and Bryk's extended version require robust and rigorous demonstrations of cause and effect. The 'gold standard' for doing that has been the RCT. The problem is that an RCT is not appropriate for DBR, for two reasons. One is an assumption we make in the LSM about the nature of schools and aggregations of schools in clusters, districts, states or even nationally. They are open and complex systems, under constant change in their participants, in their curricula and other resourcing and policy events.

The usual way to cope with this dynamic property is of course to have a large enough sample to control via randomisation. The randomisation assumes that changes that might take place in open systems will be randomly distributed. But educational and pragmatic concerns undermine acting on this assumption. The pragmatic reason is that there usually are not enough or technically could not possibly be enough districts, schools or classrooms to guarantee full randomisation, particularly in smaller nations like NZ.

But even if there were enough, the more telling concern is that average effects across schools and larger contexts are not what are important to know about. What is important is whether or not an educationally significant solution to the presenting challenge is occurring given the many expressions of the messy open systems at the level of schools, districts or larger systems. Has the change taken place at the levels required: for whom, under what conditions and to what degree of generalisation. This question becomes a pressing concern if solutions are to be tested and generalised beyond the original conditions, and certainly beyond one school and its communities. The solution to this which is described further below is to build into the various applications of the LSM as much replication as possible. Systematic replication and testing of the degree to which local solutions are generalisable are crucial to the DBR framework.

There is a related epistemological issue in the weakness of RCTs. What needs to be known from the evidence is what the 'problem' is, and what the reasonable solutions might be. This means bringing knowledge to the problem solving, even knowledge about possible curriculum-related 'packages' that are appropriate to solve the problem. But, as we discussed in earlier chapters (e.g. Chapter Two), the designs for solutions are tentative and tested and it is expected that solutions, including commodified practices from other sources, are able to be and likely to be redesigned in the light of the ongoing evidence for effectiveness in specific contexts. Given the iterative cycles, what really needs to be known is whether or not the variability in valued outcomes is shifting over time towards a more consistent and positive effect. We need to know more than what the average picture (central tendency) of the valued outcomes might be before and after a discrete intervention.

A second flaw in adopting RCTs for the purposes of establishing cause is the incompatibility with the formative process of iterative cycles of testing design and redesign. This adds to the openness of the system and its complexity. In essence, the research enterprise enters and becomes a causal entity within the system. A simple pre-treatment or pre-test followed by the experimental intervention which is followed by a post-test will not occur; the object is to get better and test and then get even more effective.

A parallel occurs in traditional clinical experiments. There the dilemma is whether there is an interaction effect between the therapist and the treatment which limits the external validity. How much of the observed change was dependent on a therapist's characteristics usually undefined and unknown, rather than the clinical treatment itself. In the case of LSM, the treatment has content too, but in a very real sense the treatment also includes the research partners as 'therapists'. How to cope with the formative properties and the partnership as influential in a research design is no easy matter. This is much more than reactivity to a measure. It is co-construction of solutions.

Counters and Criticisms.   There are various counters to this view of the limited uses of an RCT in school change. One is that the design-based enterprise should be considered more like a prototyping or trialling phase which leads to a full RCT to most rigorously establish cause. The outcome of the designing should be an educational product that is then able to be tested without change, and depending on the RCT results, taken to scale.

Another criticism is that research approaches like DBR creates a situation that may not be scalable. If the collaborative processes are part of the solving, then the partnership needs to be able to be taken to scale; it is either not cost-effective or too resource intensive. There is a related concern we have called sustainability through capability building. In the LSM, there is not the same beginning and end to a discrete intervention as would occur in a discrete RCT. Certainly there are risks of which the research design is an integral part, foremost among them making sure that there are not mutual dependencies among partners standing in the way of larger scaling up.

Each of these criticisms is important to understand and to resolve. They are potentially solvable as per our arguments about contexts and contextualisation in previous chapters. In essence, parts of the content of what is solved in any one application of the LSM may be packaged and be able to be implemented elsewhere, but this needs to take place with integrity to a process that includes the iterative collaborative analysis of data cycles. Similarly, capability building can be seen as consistent with the classic ideas from Vygotsky and the models of scaffolding (McNaughton, 2011), which propose that the social interactive plane, in our cases the partnership processes are gradually taken over by one of the partners, the schools, and built into everyday practices (a parallel to individual 'internalisation').

Our Solution: A Flexible but Robust Design

If we do not have the luxury and the simple elegance of an RCT, what are the alternatives to demonstrating causality? We innovated with this tension. In the absence of a control group of schools in the early studies of the LSM we knew there were two sources of powerful comparisons. One was with the schools themselves, and the other was with national expectations. With appropriate details and measures in place these two sources could provide answers to two driving concerns related to the local problem to be solved. The schools themselves could tell us what would have happened if we did not do anything. This would be the basis for judging statistical significance and the presence and probability of causal effects. Comparisons with the national expectations could also tell us about educational significance. In committing to equitable outcomes with excellence we needed to know whether the design, test and redesign process had accelerated learning (Chapter One), and crucially changed distributions of achievement to better match those expected nationally.

Our backgrounds in developmental and educational psychology, and literacy and language research provided these ideas. We co-opted the quasi-experimental designs of single subject research (Risley & Wolf, 1973) and repeated measures designs (Shadish, Cook, & Campbell, 2002), together with arguments about the place of formative interventions in programmatic research (McCall & Green, 2004).

In addition, we tried to meet a basic tenet of good science: the need to replicate (Sidman, 1960). Replication serves four purposes. There is the necessity to grow scientific knowledge (Popper, 1963). With replication, one can reduce the falsity content of our theories but also strengthen their truth content through successive tests and refinements of ideas (T. S. Kuhn, 1962). A second reason derives from the probabilistic nature of scientific knowledge and the need to repeat a finding so that its believability is enhanced. The third is more of a quality control argument, because 'There is many a slip twixt cupo and lip' or as Barber (1976) put it: 'there are so many pitfalls in any one experimental study that we should not take any one study too seriously' (p. 87). The final reason, particularly germane in the context of testing and retesting designs to change patterns of learning and teaching, is knowing the reliability and generality of effects including under what conditions does an intervention work (Sidman, 1960). This is the question posed by Bryk et al. and it is a heightened need in quasi-experimental research given the reduced experimental control handed over by not randomising (Borko, 2004; Chatterji, 2005; McCall & Green, 2004; Raudenbush, 2005).

The design we developed uses single-case logic within a developmental framework of cross-sectional and longitudinal data (Lai, McNaughton, Amituanai-Toloa, et al., 2009). The typical single-case design uses baseline and projection and replication. The simplest form is an A-B–A-B sequence where an intervention is added to the ongoing baseline and then subtracted in order to repeatedly show that the expected projection established by the baseline is not met, but then can be recovered. The more one does this the greater the believability. The variants of this such as multiple baseline designs use similar logic. But what we faced was a question of what could function as a 'baseline'. The usual approaches for developing baselines would not work. They were incompatible with the needs of the partnership schools to begin to work on the problem as soon as possible (and not withhold treatment for extended periods of time), or because the solutions were based on the schools sharing with and learning from each other or acting concurrently together.

Let's take the case of achievement as the valued outcome. The initial set of measures collected during the profiling is set as Time 1 (T1) and in the case of a multi-level multi-school application of the LSM can generate a cross-section of achievement across year levels. And here is the crucial first principle, the principle of expected trajectories compared with business as usual.

The cross-sectional data at T1 provide a baseline forecast of what the expected trajectory of development would be if the planned interventions had not occurred (Fig. 4). Successive stages of the intervention can then be compared with the baseline forecast and judgements about acceleration that are contextually valid can be made (Fig. 5). Repeated measures across phases, for example, at the beginning and end of each academic years and continued across years provide cohort

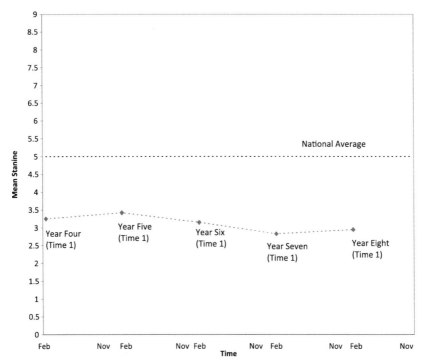

Fig. 4.   Cross-Sectional Data at Time 1 Which Shows the Achievement
Predicted for Each Year Level at the Start and End of the Year.
Source: Adapted from Lai, McNaughton, Amituanai-Toloa, et al. (2009).

longitudinal data. The obtained trajectory is systematically compared with the expected trajectory.

A second comparison is possible. Achievement measures are already used by the schools and adopted for the LSM application. Because of this the measures can be corrected for age through transformation into norm-referenced scores; they then provide an indicator of the impact of all phases against expected rates of change from national normative data thus providing us with detailed metrics for judging rates of acceleration and levels of achievement. They also provide with a means for judging effectiveness against the criterion of matching distributions.

This design, which includes replication across cohorts of students, provided us with a high degree of both internal and external validity. The internal validity comes from the in-built testing of the phased applications and the external validity comes from the systematic analysis of replication across cohorts and across schools.

This design which can be used with clusters of schools has in-built replications across age levels and across schools. These provide a series of demonstrations of possible causal relationships. However, there are possible competing explanations

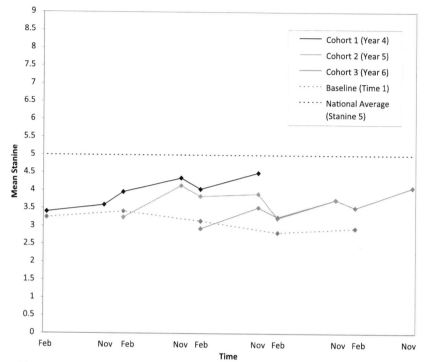

Fig. 5.   Stanine Means of Time 1–6 Cohorts against Projected Baseline.
Source: Adapted from Lai, McNaughton, Amituanai-Toloa, et al. (2009).

for the conclusions of cluster-wide results that need to be countered. These are the well-known threats to internal validity, two of which are particularly threatening in the design adopted here. The first of these major threats is that an unknown combination of factors unique to a cluster of schools – the immediate historical, cultural and social context for these particular schools – determines the outcomes; technically, this is partly an issue of ambiguous temporal precedence and partly an issue of history and maturation effects (Shadish et al., 2002). For example, the nature of students might have changed in ways that were not captured by the general descriptions of families and students, or perhaps, given that the immediate history included a number of NZ Ministry of Education initiatives the schools were developing more effective ways of teaching anyway.

A second major threat is that the students who are followed longitudinally and are continuously present over several data points are different in achievement terms from those students who are only present at T1 and subsequently left. It might be, for example, that the comparison groups contained students who were more transient and had lower achievement scores. Hence over time, as the cohort followed longitudinally is made up of just those students who are continuously and consistently at school, scores rise. This is partly an issue of potential selection bias and partly an issue of attrition (Shadish et al., 2002). As the projections on the projected baseline are based on the assumption that the students at baseline are similar to the cohort students, having a lower projected baseline may result in finding large improvements due to the design of the study, rather than any real effects.

We have found two ways of adding to the robustness of the design in addition to the in-built replications that meet the two major threats. The first is to add to the design a further innovation. To use, as a comparison, in a lagged intervention design a similar matched cluster of schools that has not received the intervention. A second way of adding to the believability of the design is by checking the characteristics of students who are included in the cross-sectional (baseline) analysis but not included in the longitudinal analysis because they were not present in subsequent repeated measures (Lai, McNaughton, Amituanai-Toloa, et al., 2009). These additions came about because we continued to treat the design itself as a problem space.

Contributing to Theoretical Knowledge

We need to know more than what worked for whom, under what conditions and at scale. We want to also know why. And we want to know why iteratively within and between any implementations of LSM. Our claim is that if we get the solution right, and know why it happened we can make contributions to our basic understandings in education. In other words, a key criterion is that the local solution has a global significance.

This is where we part ways with the original radical behaviourist underpinnings of the single-case design. In that tradition it was enough to know the conditions under which you could turn behavioural outcomes on or off, or change the rate of learning reliably. The experimental act explained the outcome. Our view is that we need technical or conceptual understandings in order for the process and/or the content of solutions to take to scale and to sustain, and to effectively generalise and adapt content and process across sites. The contextualised nature of the knowledge needs to be systematised to aid the implementation and adaptation of solutions across contexts. Two examples are provided which demonstrate our ideas of going beyond 'what works' to 'explaining'.

Example 1: Instructional Risk in the Teaching of Comprehension Strategies

In the earliest of our studies we discovered a problem in the pedagogy related to comprehension instruction. We have written about what we discovered (McNaughton & Lai, 2010). It turned out that the problem to solve was not as initially proposed, a problem of teaching reading comprehension strategies more effectively.

A theoretical contribution came about because the partnership was not fixed on a solution at the beginning. The Profiling phase was used as usual in the LSM to gather evidence of various types from a variety of sources. The patterns that emerged were paradoxical. The students' achievement data certainly indicated a problem with comprehension and with comprehension strategies and vocabulary in particular. But the classroom observation data indicated widespread and intensive strategy teaching including the evidence-based strategy of figuring our unknown words.

Through the meaning-making sessions we had with the PLCs, within the schools and across the schools, we came to the specific hypothesis that comprehension strategies were being over taught. The deliberate, explicit and repeated teaching directed students to monitor their use of strategies, reducing attention to constructing and reflecting on the meaning of the texts beyond the word level. We tested this hypothesis out in the second phase through PLD which focussed on teaching students to reflect on meanings and the sources of meaning in the texts; and elaborating word meanings through extended discourse. We could then use the repeated student assessments and classroom observations to determine if we were solving the problem and if the design for instruction for comprehension needed further modifications. It turned out that further modifications were needed. The rate of learning new words was not fast enough and needed accelerating, and ideas related to narrative and expository texts (rather than comprehending narratives per se) needed greater emphases. Among other things we redesigned the in-school and out of school practices to increase access to and use of new vocabulary.

The flexible design, and the iterative problem solving, enabled us to use the patterns in the data, and especially the paradoxical ones, to develop our ideas about solutions. These then could be conceptualised in ways that meant we could transfer the ideas to other contexts where similar patterns might suggest similar solutions, which is exactly what occurred (Lai & McNaughton, 2009). As it happens we were developing our ideas pretty much at the same time as several other research groups such as Wilkinson and Son (2010), who identified the over-teaching of strategies as a form of 'procedural display'. Our findings could be added to theirs, over time have contributed to an even more general theory of instructional risk (McNaughton, 2018)

Example 2: Explaining Digital Pedagogies

More recently, we have been working with a group of schools who are innovating with their digital environments. They serve students from the lowest socio-economic communities in NZ. They had been engaged in a digital learning initiative for several years, explicitly aimed at ameliorating the low-equity part of NZ's educational achievement profile. The initiative has established 1:1 devices, and community-wide wireless capability, enabling use at school and in homes. The programme employs digital tools for each student and promotes 'digital citizenship' inside and outside of the classroom. Although the programme employs digital tools, it is the common pedagogy which drives the professional learning in the participating schools. Collectively they employ a shared teaching approach, which they call Learn–Create–Share. Teachers create websites where students access the learning texts and tasks from school or home. Within the approach, students create (digital) artefacts to share their emerging understandings and learning with others, who offer feedback or comments. The approach is intended to support creativity and engagement in learning, as well as collaborative learning and home school links.

The LSM focus initially was posed as identifying how the pedagogy, as enacted in the classrooms was or was not accelerating learning sufficiently to meet the equity objective, and iteratively designing and redesigning for more effective pedagogy (Jesson, McNaughton, & Wilson, 2015). Like the earlier comprehension challenge, solving this turned out to be a difficult with many moving pieces. Again, the use of various measures from a variety of sources was key to the pattern detecting and the problem solving within this complexity. These included use of teacher voice data, student achievement data, student and parent questionnaires, and systematic classroom observations with contrastive classroom case studies identified through achievement data as 'pockets of promise'.

The moving parts to solve included a leadership issue. Despite teachers and students being very clear about the 1:1 goals, such as maintaining high levels of digital access, student independence and engagement, greater clarity at all levels of the schools was needed from the leaders around the shared equity goals that were the basis for meeting the acceleration challenge. The data suggested several areas for a redesign and for scaling to optimise pedagogy. One was increasing opportunities for learning and engagement. These included teachers using the affordances of the digital environment to create efficiencies, or reduced transaction costs for managing the activities in which students were engaged. Our case studies showed that in very effective classrooms teachers were design experts. Their use of very well prepared, digitalised and shared resources, enabling of high levels of students agency and the use and creation of multi-modal personalised texts freed up time to engage in high-quality interactions such as extended discussion and feedback. Other areas included the need to increase extended discussion, and instruction focussed on more complex cognitive skills, especially critical literacy.

These areas were refined over iterative cycles of collaborative analysis. We have been able over the three phases of the LSM to systematically identify and test these refinements (Jesson, McNaughton, Rosedale et al., 2018). We now know what aspects of the pedagogy are particularly important for accelerating writing achievement in these digital contexts. Two concepts elaborated from the quantitative and qualitative analyses in the application add to the literature. One is the well-known idea of implementation 'dosage'. In essence we have demonstrated again in the digital environments that the sheer amount of engagement (or dosage) with well-designed complex activities matters. We have also added to concepts about creativity and digital tools. One of the activities associated with the accelerated learning in writing was the creation of Digital Learning Objects (DLOs) based on extended reading or writing, often a co-creation by more than one author. This has enabled us to describe a pedagogy of creation activities (Jesson, McNaughton, Rosedale et al., 2018). Moreover, these two ideas are connected. The reading of multiple texts, and synthesis and differentiation achieved through creating DLOs, increases the dosage, specifically in the area of the cognitive complexity of independent activity and impacts on writing achievement. As with the previous example, related findings are emerging internationally. In this case international studies are finding evidence for the importance of multiple text synthesis through co-creation of written products (Killi & Leu, 2019)

By What Mechanisms Do We Learn to Become Better?

We have learned how to learn within the LSM application. Not just about the content from iterations within an application but also about that content across successive applications. For example, the early learning about comprehension and the need for rich discourse-based comprehending has been elaborated and refined in successive applications which have the same or a similar focus. So in a more recent study of secondary literacy we extended our understanding of the role of discourse and comprehension in a blended view of adolescent literacy (Lai et al., 2014). Both generic and content-area literacy skills and knowledge, that is the generalisable literacy skills and knowledge and those specific to a content-area such as mathematics, are important and every content-area-based reading and writing task will involve students' generic and content-area literacy knowledge. Even more recently we have developed a model of instructional practice in literacy that can span primary and secondary year levels which builds on the early ideas of complexity and practice (Wilson & Oldehaver, 2017). It is a view of reading both wide (across exemplars) and deep (intensive study of a core text). And resources can be bundled which provide examples that are challenging in complexity, moderate or relatively easy and these fulfil different functions.

There are many examples of our learning more about the processes involved in the LSM. The idea of systematically using variability to identify outliers and studying those as cases was incipient in our initial studies. But we learned from those initial studies that this was key to developing more effective designs. Often as not capability already existed in the contexts and by understanding these 'pockets of promise' we could develop more robust purpose-built and sustainable designs.

Another example is that earlier applications of the LSM assumed a three phase A, A+B, A+ C design, where A is collaborative analysis of data, B is resourcing and C is sustainability. Through subsequent iterations of the LSM across contexts, we come to realise that B (the resourcing) does not stop, rather the design is additive where the final phase is A+B+C. We also come to realise that our original ideas of B being professional development did not encapsulate all that occurred in those phases, and thus the terminology was changed.

How is this knowledge building possible? It is possible because the LSM involves deliberate thinking deployed in structured collaborative activities, through which ideas are formed and reformed as hypotheses, and are tested and retested. These collaborative activities develop collective as well as hybridised forms of knowledge, meaning more nuanced forms of evidence-informed practice. The second reason is that the LSM is heavy on both process and on content. Finally, we consider learning through partnership loops and the dispositions to learn through them as important for knowledge building. In this last section, we outline the mechanisms by which we can learn to solve problems of practice, and through which we can extend our knowledge.

Thinking and Testing Ideas

There are fundamental cognitive and reasoning processes that sit behind the LSM activities which can produce increasingly better designs and new knowledge. These processes are evident in the key LSM concepts and their associated processes, that is, collaborative analysis of data and contextualisation of effective practice to local contexts.

In 2011, Daniel Kahneman summarised much of what we know about thinking into two basic systems he called fast and slow. The fast system (System 1) operates near automatically and quickly, with little effortful control and the second allocates attention to effortful mental activities that demand it. All of us, including researchers, teachers and leaders, build up System 1 responses so that our moment by moment decisions and choices require little effort and conscious control. But the second system is needed to override working choices and immediate responses. It is needed if we are to test the veracity and usefulness of our assumptions and decisions.

It is this second system interacting with the first that gives us the potential to develop knowledge and skills. These interactions are evident in how we designed the collaborative analysis of data and associated contextualisation of effective practice to local contexts. In each case, there is both the fast system of identifying what the problem that the partnership is trying to solve might be, most evident in the initial raising of hypotheses and possible solutions. However, rather than act on System 1 ideas, the collaborative analysis of data process forces every fast system idea to be slowed down and systematically tested against available evidence (see e.g. Chapters Two and Three). This process is done collaboratively. This adds value as partners with different knowledge critique existing ideas and diverse (and sometimes contradictory) ideas from partners are raised, both of which serve to reduce confirmation bias. Similarly, through the process of contextualisation, known effective practices that may come from System 1 responses based on years of experience are tested against evidence from the local context.

Reasoning 'Up and Down'.   Applied in the LSM process Kahneman's second system contain elements of both inductive and deductive reasoning. The various measures across a range of sources provide patterns, and through effortful attention to confirming patterns and the discordances, we induce likely explanations. But interacting with this process is the network of concepts about learning, teaching and development and empirical knowledge which give meaning to the patterns. Both researchers and educators bring to the partnerships sets of knowledge and skills that are the basis for thinking both from the ground up and from principles. The frames of reference partners have filter and accentuate what evidence might be needed to best understand the context and its challenges.

Our science has a knowledge base and thanks to that accumulated knowledge some things are known. For example, among the core components of effective pedagogy is feedback and we know a lot about its role in learning (Hattie & Timperley, 2007). There are principles about timing, the focus and about the relationships with 'feedforward'. But anticipating what we say below about the critical role of collective and hybridised knowledge, there is a piece we often do not know. What we often do not know is how the core properties of instruction are enacted in the complex time-restricted contexts of classrooms, let alone in a particular classroom, with particular learners, at a particular time in a particular activity. This is a question of how a working concept needs to be contextualised (Chapters Two and Three).

A striking example of this tension between generalised principle and local context is how it has proved punishingly difficult to shift classroom discourse from the default condition of IRE sequences to more extensive use of dialogic forms. The significance of dialogue is well known and there are well-developed theoretical models (Wilkinson & Son, 2010). Similarly, the limited usefulness of IRE (teacher initiates a question, student responds and the teacher evaluates the answer) sequences in learning is well known and there are principles that explain those limitations (Cazden, 2001). But the mechanisms for teachers being able to engage in dialogue consistently and efficiently and at scale are still to be solved.

So being able to understand local context from the ground up but armed with principles and accumulated knowledge is key. This is why a key concept underpinning our work is contextualising known effective practices to local contexts, and the processes we have developed in the LSM around collaborative analysis of data and contextualising of effective practice are so important (Chapter Two). We enter into the activities of meaning-making with sufficiently open minds to be able to consider a range of hypotheses and explanations. Local knowledge and local solutions are serious contenders for these working hypotheses, the task being to exclude the least likely and entertain the most likely given the available evidence from the local context and the principled knowledge.

Reasoning Like.   Analogical reasoning has a role too. From a research perspective there is a constant checking of how the local situation is like or not like other situations. The reasoning goes, if the current situation and its challenge are like another one we have experienced, it should share certain features. In Chapter Three, for example, the extended example showed how the two clusters of schools had similar issues with students' vocabulary knowledge and similar teaching practices (like situation), but that we also found some critical differences in teaching practices in the second group of schools that influenced the solutions that were developed for that cluster of schools and subsequent schools.

Reasoning with Soft Skills: Thinking Collectively.   There are so-called 'soft skills', particularly those associated with self-control and critical reasoning. Despite being considered 'soft' and sometimes even called 'non-cognitive' (Kautz, Heckman, Diris, ter Weel, & Borghans, 2015), they nevertheless involve complex cognitive processes. Core features of self-control are certainly identifiable in the activities of developing and testing and retesting in a partnership. That is, being able to attend to and maintain attention to the critical elements of what is being proposed, as well as persevering in looking for and using requisite evidence (Duckworth & Steinberg, 2015). Similarly, we all default easily to confirmatory bias, looking for evidence that corroborates or is consistent with one's existing views. It takes these aspects of self-control to work through alternative explanations and hypotheses. It also takes considerable self-control to reject favoured solutions or stop doing something that is not working.

But in addition to intrapersonal skills, interpersonal skills are required. As we discussed in Chapter Four, partnerships require interpersonal skills based on awareness and understanding of, and respect for others' knowledge and doing so in a culturally appropriate way. Empathy and perspective taking are therefore needed to engage with others in considering alternatives and entertaining possible solutions, even if they are not one's own proposals or preferences. Being able to argue in ways that are considerate of others' positions and acting in ways that do not undermine ensure activities are reciprocal and knowledge can be co-constructed. The processes of collaborative analysis of data to develop shared hypotheses entail forms of argumentation or collaborative reasoning. Advanced levels entail these interpersonal skills and they are needed for understanding other's positions and adjusting one's own (D. Kuhn, 2015).

Reasoning How and That.   We have learned that high levels of both process and content are needed. Another way to put this is that declarative (akin to content) and procedural (akin to process) knowledge are involved to high levels and there are two senses of treatment integrity which this commitment entails. The integrity of the process is important. We need to be able to consistently and accurately carry out activities which we know are needed for making meaning and designing and testing solutions.

But process without well-articulated knowledge is at best vacuous. We know that being able to solve problems depends on both strategies and content-area knowledge, and the literature on expertise indicates that experts have acquired a great deal of content knowledge that is organised in ways that reflect deep understanding of their subject (Bransford et al., 2000). Unfortunately, educational interventions tend to emphasise one or the other. But here we emphasise both in every aspect of the LSM, for example, in our collaborative analysis of data, where we emphasise the important of content-area knowledge, in particular PCK, in the process (Chapter Three) and as important expertise required for the partnership to function effectively (Chapter Four).

There are two implications from this conclusion for the membership of partnerships. The content knowledge held by the research partners, just like the content knowledge of school partners, will tend to filter the problem definition. It is perhaps not surprising, given the presence of internationally renowned researchers in vocabulary and language that the SERP applications have produced extraordinary designs that are related to vocabulary and comprehension (Snow, 2015). Similarly, it is not surprising that a number of the applications of Improvement Science reported by Bryk, who is a leading international authority on the organisational and social properties of schools, are to do with solving structural properties of school systems. Having such expertise is not negative in itself, as such expertise allows for a deep analysis of the problem to be solved.

As such, the first implication is that process needs to be robust enough to be informed by, but not dictated to by the specific content-area expertise of the research members. We have discussed this in Chapter Three, where we provide a caveat on the LSM focusses to date based on our collective expertise, but also demonstrated how the processes built into the LSM help mitigate such inherent preferences. The second is that purpose-built teams are needed in the models like the LSM.

Feedback Loops and Associated Disposition

A core process we uncovered for being able to learn on the job is the role of partnerships in providing feedback and feedforward loops. These loops are basic and well-known processes, at both an individual and a collective level. But it is the role of the partnerships and our networks that enable (or constrain) how salient the feedback is and how well we can learn from them. Associated with this is a second process, preparedness to learn from our actions and from others. This may seem obvious, but it is a property that is not often associated with the application of research expertise to an intervention. More often than not, the application is one of not being tentative, rather being fixed on the testing of an already firmed up hypothesis. The results of the application might then demand rethinking. A third process is deliberate problem solving at all levels. That is, treating the methods adopted and the solutions tested as problem spaces in their own right.

A simple example here will exemplify what we mean. At one point in the second phase of an application of the LSM when we had been feeding back the latest achievement data, leaders of school clusters argued that the lower than desired rates of gain were likely the result of problematic rates of absence. As we have explained elsewhere in this book the emergence of a new hypothesis and an iterative modification in focus is not uncommon. In this case, it came somewhat 'out of the blue', not having been raised in the first phase. More difficult, it required an unplanned expenditure of time and resource to systematically check the relationships between absences and achievement. But the reciprocal partnership obligations and protocols (previously refereed to using the Māori concept of a whānau of interest) were such that the expenditure was needed.

No matter which way we ran the data however, we could not find a straightforward relationship between absences and achievement and the data looked as though the absentee rate was probably better than some other schools. We fed this 'non-result' back at several school and cluster-level meetings. Some weeks later we heard from the schools that the truancy officers employed by the NZ Ministry of Education had been very upset. The message they had heard was that academics had said that being absent from school did not matter. What we learned again, was that the message matters. We needed to nuance the message so that it was clear what we were saying and what we were not, could not or should not say. What we were saying was that given the levels and rates, absences were not a major reason for the current rates of achievement. But more importantly, the message needed to say that being at school may be very important for other reasons and not being at school, for example, hanging around the local streets, might very well be problematic, for other reasons.

We could not have learned more about the nature of messaging without the trusted processes of feedback that had built up in the partnership and our preparedness to 'hear' the feedback. The meta-part of this was that we learned that we need to learn about how messages are received and possible interpretations. The messages themselves are a problem space. We have built this sense of being empathetic, or anticipating possible effects into our processes by interrogating the possibilities prior to a major session in which we are presenting data, and even by role playing likely reactions.

What Do We Still Need to Learn?

We started this book identifying five big challenges facing educational interventions aimed at increasing the effectiveness of schooling systems. These were identified as variability, scalability, capability, acceleration and sustainability. These challenges are especially stark if the need to be more effective is for those students from low socio-economic and culturally diverse communities traditionally not well served by schools.

We have learned a lot about how these challenges might be solved with practice-embedded research approaches such as the LSM. In each of the chapters, there are examples of partial or emerging solutions. We are confident that practice-embedded research approaches more generally and design-based approaches like the LSM more specifically are better able to deliver solutions to the pressing challenges facing schools. In various ways, groups like ourselves are responding to Snow's (2015) call to be better at solving educational issues through our sciences.

Given we claim that applications of the LSM have a knowledge-building function, we end the chapters with thoughts on what we still need to learn. Variability poses a conundrum. On the one hand, variability in effectiveness in a system allows us to identify pockets of effectiveness in context. But interventions, or in our case applications of the LSM, are notorious for having variable impact. We need to know better how to manage this balancing act. Solving this requires more precise understanding of properties of the collective solving as well as the 'dosages' or 'intensities' with which partnerships need to function. The question to answer is what is the variability that is acceptable in order to guarantee the valued outcomes such as accelerated learning and distributions of achievement which match national expectations for at-risk groups.

Scalability and sustainability are perennial problem, especially in a system such as NZ's which values autonomy of schools, supports teachers to design local curricula and has a history of teachers engaged in solving problems in situ. A partnership approach like the LSM adds considerable complexity to thinking about scalability and sustainability. There are a number of possible directions that solutions could take. One is thinking of partnerships as meta-system versions of scaffolds and zones of proximal development. The partnership has a function to transfer capability to the schools. But we have also argued that ongoing solving requires research input alongside the expertise required for that capability. If engaging in partnerships is a more effective way of solving real educational issues and can deliver scientific knowledge, then the question becomes how to create and maintain partnerships at scale. The idea of co-operative but flexible hubs as proposed by Bryk et al. (2015) is an organisational solution. This in turn requires rethinking the role, functions and funding of university research groupings and the nature of valued research.

Capability building also requires us to better understand the nature of resourcing for developing professional knowledge and skills. There is a large literature on resourcing, and in particular PLD. But as we have noted in this book, we do not yet fully understand what is necessary to build capability that improves valued student outcomes and is sustainable. In our view capability means both generative PCK and instructional design knowledge appropriate for solving the immediate challenges, and also process knowledge. It is also how to engage in data discussions and how to be effective in drawing out testable hypotheses that most reasonably fit the evidence. Building capability will need to do so in all these areas.

Finally, there are still things to be learned about how to make educationally significant differences for students who have traditionally not been as well served by schools. The criterion of accelerated learning which can produce the matched distributions is unforgiving. In successive applications, we learnt that we can achieve the criterion within a school year, but then the well-known summer learning effect reduced the gains when considered year on year (Jesson, McNaughton, Wilson et al., 2018). Having solved one part of the problem we have now needed to solve another part which is more about educational capital and community engagement. We have also found as others have that a successful focus on one content-area such as writing does not result in similar levels of gains in others, even in reading. There are obvious reasons for this such as instructional focus and opportunity costs (McNaughton, 2018). But slow solving of one subject area after another has been identified by our partners as a problem space also.

There is more to learn. But practice-embedded research approaches and more specifically DBR-type approaches such as the LSM are always learning. It is this capacity to learn in partnership with others that makes us confident that the LSM can deliver on the promise of better outcomes for students.

References

Alozie, N. M., Moje, E. B., & Krajcik, J. S. (2010). An analysis of the supports and constraints for scientific discussion in high school project-based science. *Science Education, 94*(3), 395–427.

Anderson, T., & Shattuck, J. (2012). Design-based research: A decade of progress in education research? *Educational Researcher, 41*(1), 16–25. doi:10.3102/0013189X11428813

Argyris, C. (1982). *Reasoning, learning and action: Individual and organizational.* San Francisco, CA: Jossey-Bass.

Bandura, A. (1995). Exercise of personal and collective efficacy in changing societies. In A. Bandura (Ed.), *Self-efficacy in changing societies* (pp. 1–45). Cambridge: Cambridge University Press.

Barber, T. X. (1976). *Pitfalls in human research: Ten pivotal points.* New York, NY: Pergamon.

Berryman, M., Lawrence, D., & Lamont, R. (2018). Cultural relationships for responsive pedagogy: A bicultural mana orite perspective. Retrieved from https://www.nzcer.org.nz/system/files/journals/set/downloads/2018_1_003_1.pdf

Biemiller, A. (1999). *Language and reading success.* Cambridge, MA: Brookline.

Bishop, R. (2011). *Freeing ourselves* (Vol. 66). Rotterdam: Sense Publishers.

Block, C. C., & Pressley, M. (Eds.). (2002). *Comprehension instruction: Research-based best practices.* New York, NY: Guilford Press.

Bolam, R., McMahon, A., Stoll, L., Thomas, S., & Wallace, M. (2005). *Creating and sustaining effective learning communities.* Bristol: University of Bristol.

Borko, H. (2004). Professional development and teacher learning: Mapping the terrain. *Educational Researcher, 33*(8), 3–15.

Borman, G. D. (2005). National efforts to bring reform to scale in high-poverty schools: Outcomes and implications. In L. Parker (Ed.), *Review of research in education* (Vol. 29, pp. 1–28). Washington, DC: American Educational Research Association.

Bransford, J. D., Brown, A. L., & Cocking, R. R. (2000). *How people learn: Brain, mind, experience, and school.* Washington, DC: National Academy Press.

Bronfenbrenner, U. (1979). *The ecology of human development: Experiments by nature and design.* Cambridge, MA: Harvard University Press.

Brown, A. L. (1992). Design experiments: Theoretical and methodological challenges in creating complex interventions in classroom settings. *The Journal of the Learning Sciences, 2*(2), 141–178.

Brown, C., & Poortman, C. L. (Eds.). (2018). *Networks for learning: Effective collaboration for teacher, school and system improvement.* Abingdon: Routledge Taylor & Francis Group.

Bryk, A. S., Gomez, L. M., Grunow, A., & LeMahieu, P. G. (2015). *Learning to improve: How America's schools can get better at getting better.* Cambridge, MA: Harvard Education Press.

Buly, M. R., & Valencia, S. W. (2002). Below the bar: Profiles of students who fail state reading assessments. *Educational Evaluation and Policy Analysis, 24*(3), 219–239. doi:10.3102/01623737024003219

Carlson, D., Borman, G. D., & Robinson, M. (2011). A multistate district-level cluster randomized trial of the impact of data-driven reform on reading and mathematics achievement. *Educational Evaluation and Policy Analysis, 33*(3), 378–398. http:// dx.doi.org/10.3102/0162373711412765

Cazden, C. (2001). *Classroom discourse: The language of teaching and learning* (2nd ed.). Portsmouth: Heinemann.

Centre for Data-Driven Reform in Education. (2011). Achievement planning: Solutions. Retrieved from http://www.cddre.org/achievement/solutions.html. Accessed on February 24, 2016.

Chatterji, M. (2005). Achievement gaps and correlates of early mathematics achievement: Evidence from the ECLS K-first grade sample. *Education Policy Analysis Archives, 13*(45), 1–38.

Clay, M. M. (1993). *Reading recovery*. Auckland: Heinemann.

Clay, M. M. (2013). *An observation survey of early literacy achievement*. Auckland: Heinemann.

Coalition for Evidence-Based Policy. (2013). Randomized controlled trials commissioned by the Institute of Education Sciences since 2002: How many found positive versus weak or no effects. Retrieved from http://coalition4evidence.org/wp-content/uploads/2013/06/ IES-Commissioned-RCTs-positive-vs-weak-or-null-findings-7-2013.pdf

Cobb, P., Confrey, J., diSessa, A., Lehrer, R., & Schauble, L. (2003). Design experiments in educational research. *Educational Researcher, 32*(1), 9–13.

Cobb, P., Jackson, K., Smith, T., Sorum, M., & Henrik, E. (2013). Design research with educational systems: Investigating and supporting improvements in the quality of mathematics teaching and learning at scale. *National Society for the Study of Education Yearbook, 112*(2), 320–349.

Coburn, C. (2003). Rethinking scale: Moving beyond numbers to deep and lasting change. *Educational Researcher, 32*(6), 3–12

Coburn, C. E., & Penuel, W. R. (2016). Research-practice partnerships in education: Outcomes, dynamics and open questions. *Educational Researcher, 45*(1), 48–54. doi:10.3102/0013189X16631750

Coburn, C. E., Penuel, W. R., & Geil, K. (2013). *Research-practice partnerships at the district level: A new strategy for leveraging research for educational improvement*. New York, NY: William T. Grant Foundation.

Cooper, H., Charlton, K., Valentine, J. C. & Muhlenbruck, L. (2000). Making the most of Summer school: A meta analytic and narrative review. *Monographs of the Society for Research in Child Development, 260*(65), 1–52.

Cuban, L. (2003). *Why is it so hard to get good schools?* New York, NY: Teachers College Press.

Darling-Hammond, L., & Bransford, J. (2005). *Preparing teachers for a changing world: What teachers should learn and be able to do*. San Francisco, CA: Jossey-Bass.

Darling-Hammond, L., & Richardson, N. (2009). Teacher learning: What matters? *Educational Leadership, 66*(5), 46–53.

Datnow, A. (2005). The sustainability of comprehensive school reform models in changing district and state contexts. *Educational Administration Quarterly, 41*(1), 121–153. doi:10.1177/0013161X04269578

Datnow, A., Borman, G., Stringfield, S., Overman, L., & Castellano, M. (2003). Comprehensive school reform in culturally and linguistically diverse contexts: Implementation and outcomes from a 4-year study. *Educational Evaluation and Policy Analysis, 25*, 143–170.

Design-Based Research Collective. (2003). Design-based research: An emerging paradigm for educational inquiry. *Educational Researcher, 32*(1), 5–8.

Duckworth, A. L., & Steinberg, L. (2015). Unpacking self-control. *Child Development Perspectives, 9*(1), 32–37.

Durlak, J. A., & DuPre, E. P. (2008). Implementation matters: A review of research on the influence of implementation on program outcomes and the factors affecting implementation. *American Journal of Community Psychology, 41*(3–4), 327. doi:10.1007/s10464-008-9165-0

Earl, L., & Katz, S. (2006). *Leading in a data rich world.* Thousand Oaks, CA: Corwin Press.

Earl, L., & Timperley, H. (Eds.). (2008). *Evidence-based conversations to improve educational practices.* Dordrecht, The Netherlands: Kluwer/Springer Academic Publishers.

Eglash, R. (1999). *African fractals: Modern computing and indigenous design.* New Brunswick, NJ: Rutgers University Press.

Elley, W. (2001). *STAR supplementary test of achievement in reading: Years 4–6.* Wellington: New Zealand Council for Educational Research.

Ericsson, A. K., & Pool, R. (2016). *Peak: Secrets from the new science of expertise.* New York, NY: Houghton Mifflin Harcourt.

Fernandez, C., & Yoshida, M. (2012). *A Japanese approach to improving mathematics teaching and learning.* New York, NY: Routledge.

Fjørtoft, H., & Lai, M. K. (2019). Affordances of narrative and numerical data for data teams: A social-semiotic approach to data use. Paper presented at the American Educational Research Association Conference, Toronto, Canada.

Frederiksen, N. (1984). Implications of cognitive theory for instruction in problem solving. *Review of Educational Research, 54*(3), 363–407. https://doi.org/10.2307/1170453.

Fullan, M., Rincon-Gallardo, S., & Hargreaves, A. (2015). Professional capital as accountability. *Education Policy Analysis Archives, 23*(15), 1–17.

Fulton, F., Doerr, H., & Britton, T. (2010). *STEM teachers in professional learning communities: A knowledge synthesis.* Washington, DC: National Commission on Teaching & America's Future & West Ed.

Garet, M. S., Porter, A. C., Desimone, L., Birman, B. F., & Yoon, K. S. (2001). What makes professional development effective? Results from a national sample of teachers. *American Educational Research Journal, 38*(4), 915–945.

Gilbert, J. (2005). *Educational issues for communities affected by transience and residential mobility.* Wellington: New Zealand Council for Educational Research.

Groenke, S. (2010). Missed opportunities, misunderstandings, and misgivings: A case study analysis of three beginning English teachers' attempts at authentic discussion with adolescents in a synchronous CMC environment. *Journal of Technology and Teacher Education, 18*(3), 387–414.

Gummer, E., & Mandinach, E. (2015). Building a conceptual framework for data literacy. *Teachers College Record, 117*(4), 1–22.

Guskey, T. R. (2003). What makes professional development effective? *Phi Delta Kappan, 84,* 748–750. http://dx.doi.org/10.1177/003172170308401007

Halverson, R. (2003). Systems of practice: How leaders use artifacts to create professional community in schools. *Education Policy Analysis Archives, 11*(37), 1–35. doi: 11.10.14507/epaa.v11n37.2003

Hart, B., & Risley, T. R. (1995). *Meaningful differences in the everyday experience of young American children.* Baltimore, MD: P. H. Brookes.

Hatano, G., & Inagaki, K. (1986). Two courses of expertise. In H. Stevenson, H. Azuma, & K. Hakuta (Eds.), *Children development and education in Japan* (pp. 262–272). New York, NY: Freeman.

Hattie, J. (2009). *Visible learning: A synthesis of over 800 meta-analyses relating to achievement.* Abingdon: Routledge Taylor & Francis Group.

Hattie, J., Brown, G. T. L., Keegan, P. J., MacKay, A. J., Irving, S. E., Cutforth, S., … Yu, J. (2005). *Assessment tools for teaching and learning (asTTle) version 4: Manual.* Wellington: University of Auckland.

Hattie, J., & Timperley, H. (2007). The power of feedback. *Review of Educational Research, 77*(1), 81–112. https://doi.org/10.3102/003465430298487

Hawley, W. D., & Valli, L. (1999). The essentials of effective professional development: A new consensus. In L. Darling-Hammond & G. Sykes (Eds.), *Teaching as a learning profession* (pp. 127–150). San Francisco, CA: Jossey-Bass.

Hunzicker, J. (2011). Effective professional development for teachers: A checklist. *Professional Development in Education, 37*(2), 177–179. doi:10.1080/19415257.2010.523955

Jesson, R., McNaughton, S., Rosedale, N., Zhu, T., & Cockle, V. (2018). A mixed-methods study to identify effective practices in the teaching of writing in a digital learning environment in low income schools. *Computers and Education, 119*(April), 14–30.

Jesson, R., McNaughton, S., & Wilson, A. (2015). Raising literacy levels using digital learning: A design-based approach in New Zealand. *The Curriculum Journal, 26*(2), 198–223. doi:10.1080/09585176.2015.1045535

Jesson, R., McNaughton, S., Wilson, A., Zhu, T., & Cockle, V. (2018): Improving achievement using digital pedagogy: Impact of a research practice partnership in New Zealand. *Journal of Research on Technology in Education, 50*(3), 183–199. doi:10.1080/15391523.2018.1436012

Jones, S. M., LaRusso, M., Kim, J., Kim, H Y, Selman, R., Uccelli, P., … Snow, C. (2019). Experimental effects of Word Generation on vocabulary, academic language, perspective taking, and reading comprehension in high poverty schools. *Journal of Research in Educational Effectiveness, 12*, 448–483. https://doi.org/10.1080/19345747.2019.1615155

Kahneman, D. (2011). *Thinking, fast and slow*. London: Penguin Books.

Kautz, T., Heckman J. J., Diris, R., ter Weel, B., & Borghans, L. (2015). Fostering and measuring skills: Improving cognitive and non-cognitive skills to promote lifetime success. Retrieved from http://www.oecd.org/education/ceri/Fostering-and-Measuring-Skills-Improving-Cognitive-and-Non-Cognitive-Skills-to-Promote-Lifetime-Success.pdf

Kennedy, A. (2005). Models of continuing professional development: A framework for analysis. *Journal of In-Service Education, 31*(2), 235–250.

Kennedy, M. M. (1998). Form and Substance in Inservice Teacher Education (Research Monograph No. 13). Wisconsin, USA: The National Institute for Science Education, University of Wisconsin-Madison. Retrieved from https://msu.edu/~mkennedy/publications/docs/Teacher%20Learning/NISE/Kennedy%20effects%20of%20PD.pdf.

Killi, C., & Leu, D. J. (2019). Exploring the collaborative synthesis of information during online reading. *Computers in Human Behavior, 95*, 146–157.

Kuhn, D. (2015). Thinking together and alone. *Educational Researcher, 44*(1), 46–53.

Kuhn, T. S. (1962). *The structure of scientific revolutions*. Chicago, IL: University of Chicago Press.

Lai, M. K. (2019). Learning networks to sustain literacy interventions. Paper presented at the American Educational Research Association Conference, Toronto, Canada.

Lai, M. K., & Kushner, S. (2013). *A developmental and negotiated approach to school self-evaluation* (Vol. 14). Bingley: Emerald Publishing.

Lai, M. K., & McNaughton, S. (2009). Not by achievement analysis alone: How inquiry needs to be informed by evidence from classrooms. *New Zealand Journal of Educational Studies, 44*(2), 93–108.

Lai, M. K., & McNaughton, S. (2016). The impact of data use professional development on student achievement. *Teaching and Teacher Education, 60*, 434–443. doi:10.1016/j.tate.2016.07.005

Lai, M. K., & McNaughton, S. (2018). Learning networks for sustainable literacy achievement. In C. Brown & C. L. Poortman (Eds.), *Networks for learning: Effective collaboration for teacher, school and system improvement* (pp. 152–171). Abingdon: Routledge Taylor & Francis Group. doi:10.4324/9781315276649

Lai, M. K., McNaughton, S., Amituanai-Toloa, M., Turner, R., & Hsiao, S. (2009). Sustained acceleration of achievement in reading comprehension: The New Zealand experience. *Reading Research Quarterly, 44*(1), 30–56. doi:10.1598/RRQ.44.1.2

Lai, M. K., McNaughton, S., & Hsiao, S. (2011). Does 'it' last? Sustainability of literacy interventions. In J. Parr, H. Hedges, & S. May (Eds.), *Changing trajectories of teaching and learning* (pp. 219–244). Wellington: New Zealand Council for Educational Research.

Lai, M. K., McNaughton, S., Macdonald, S. D., & Farry, S. J. (2004). Profiling reading comprehension in Mangere schools: A research and development collaboration. *New Zealand Journal of Educational Studies, 2004*(39), 223–240.

Lai, M. K., McNaughton, S., Timperley, H. S., & Hsiao, S. (2009). Sustaining continued acceleration in reading comprehension achievement following an intervention. *Educational Assessment, Evaluation and Accountability, 21*(1), 81–100. doi:10.1007/s11092-009-9071-5

Lai, M. K., & Schildkamp, K. (2013). Data-based decision making: An overview. In K. Schildkamp, M. K. Lai, & L. Earl (Eds.), *Data-based decision making around the world: Challenges and opportunities* (pp. 9–21). Netherlands: Springer.

Lai, M. K., & Schildkamp, K. (2016). In-service teacher professional learning: Use of assessment in data-based decision-making. In G. T. Brown & L. Harris (Eds.), *Handbook of human and social conditions in assessment* (pp. 77–94). New York, NY: Routledge.

Lai, M. K., Wilson, A., McNaughton, S., & Hsiao, S. (2014). Improving achievement in secondary schools: Impact of a literacy project on reading comprehension and secondary school qualifications. *Reading Research Quarterly, 49*(3), 305–334. doi:10.1002/rrq.73

Lipman, P. (1997). Restructuring in context: A case study of teacher participation and the dynamics of ideology, race, and power. *American Educational Research Journal, 34*(1), 3–37. https://doi.org/10.3102/00028312034001003

Little, J. (2003). Inside teacher community: Representations of classroom practice. *Teachers College Record, 105*(6), 913–945.

Marsh, J. A. (2012). Interventions promoting educators' use of Data: Research insights and gaps. *Teachers College Record, 114*(11), 1–48.

May, H., Goldsworthy, H., Armijo, M., Gray, A., Sirinides, P., Blalock, T. J., … Sam, C. (2014). CRPE year 2 report 2012–2013: Evaluation of the i3 scale-up of reading recovery. Retrieved from http://www.cpre.org/sites/default/files/researchreport/2036_rryear2report.pdf

May, H., Sirinides, P., Gray, A., & Goldsworthy, H. (2016). *Reading recovery: An evaluation of the four-year i3 scale-up.* Philadelphia, PA: Consortium for Policy Research in Education.

McCall, R. B., & Green, B. L. (2004). Beyond the methodological gold standards of behavior research: Considerations for policy and practice. *Social Policy Report, 28*(2), 1–19.

McNaughton, S. (2001). 'A beneficial interest?' Learning and teaching in native schools. In J. Simon & L. T. Smith (Eds.), *A civilising mission? Perceptions and representations of the New Zealand native schools system* (pp. 89–140). Auckland: Auckland University Press.

McNaughton, S. (2002). *Meeting of minds.* Wellington: Learning Media.

McNaughton, S. (2011). *Designing better schools for culturally and linguistically diverse children: A science of performance model for research.* New York, NY: Routledge.

McNaughton, S. (2014). Classroom instruction: The influences of Marie Clay. *The Reading Teacher, 68*(2), 88–92. doi:10.1002/trtr.1286

McNaughton, S. (2017). Solving pressing challenges: The role of a lead teacher. In R. Jesson, A. Wilson, S. McNaughton., & M. Lai (Eds.), *Teachers leading inquiry for school problem solving* (pp. 4–8). Wellington: New Zealand Council for Educational Research.

McNaughton, S. (2018). *Instructional risk in education: Why instruction can fail.* New York, NY: Routledge.

McNaughton, S., & Lai, M. K. (2008). *Raising a region's literacy levels: A technical report on the West Coast Literacy Project.* Auckland: Auckland Uniservices Ltd.

McNaughton, S., & Lai, M. K. (2010). The learning schools model of school change to raise achievement in reading comprehension for culturally and linguistically diverse students in New Zealand. In P. H. Johnston (Ed.), *RTI in literacy – Responsive and comprehensive* (pp. 313–336). Newark: International Reading Association.

McNaughton, S., Lai, M. K., & Hsiao, S. (2012). Testing the effectiveness of an intervention model based on data use: A replication series across clusters of schools. *School Effectiveness and School Improvement, 23*(2), 203–228. doi:10.1080/09243453.2011. 652126

Ministry of Education. (2007). *The New Zealand curriculum for English-medium teaching and learning in years 1–13.* Wellington: Ministry of Education.

Ministry of Education (n.d.-a). Your school board of trustees. Retrieved from https:// parents.education.govt.nz/primary-school/getting-involved-in-your-childs-school/ your-school-board-of-trustees/

Ministry of Education. (n.d.-b). Reporting to parents and whanau. Retrieved from http:// assessment.tki.org.nz/Reporting-to-parents-whanau/Clarifications-about-National-Standards

Ministry of Education. (n.d.-c). Māori achieving success as Māori – MASAM. Retrieved from http://elearning.tki.org.nz/Leadership/Maori-achieving-success-as-Maori

Ministry of Education. (n.d.-d). Communities of learning. Retrieved from https://www. education.govt.nz/further-education/communities-of-learning-kahui-ako-informa-tion-for-postsecondary-education-and-training-providers/

Nair, B., Smart, W., & Smyth, R. (2007). How does investment in tertiary education improve outcomes. *Social Policy Journal, 31*, 195–217. Retrieved from https://www.msd. govt.nz/about-msd-and-our-work/publications-resources/journals-and-magazines/ social-policy-journal/spj31/31-how-does-investment-in-tertiary-education-improve-outcomes-pages195-217.html

National Research Council. (2003). *Strategic education research partnership.* Washington, DC: National Academies Press. https://doi.org/10.17226/10670

Newmann, F., Smith, B., Allensworth, E., & Bryk, S. (2001). Instructional program coherence: What it is and why it should guide school improvement policy. *Educational Evaluation and Policy Analysis, 23*(4), 297–321.

OECD. (2013). Education policy outlook snapshot: New Zealand. Retrieved from http:// www.oecd.org/newzealand/highlightsnewzealand.htm

OECD. (2015). PISA 2015 results: Excellence and equity in education. doi:10.1787/ 9789264266490-en. Retrieved from https://read.oecd-ilibrary.org/education/pisa-2015-results-volume-i_9789264266490-en#page5

Palincsar, A. S., & Brown, A. L. (1984). Reciprocal teaching of comprehension-fostering and comprehension-monitoring activities. *Cognition and Instruction, 1*(2), 117–175. doi:10.1207/s1532690xci0102_1

Peurach, D. J. (2016). Innovating at the nexus of impact and improvement: Leading educational improvement networks. *Educational Researcher, 45*(7), 421–429. doi:10.31 02/0013189X16670898

Popper, K. R. (1963). *Conjectures and refutations: The growth of scientific knowledge.* London: Routledge & K. Paul.

Pressley, M. (2000). What should comprehension instruction be the instruction of? In M. L. Kamil, P. B. Mosenthal, P. D. Pearson, & R. Barr (Eds.), *Handbook of reading research* (Vol. 3, pp. 545–561). Mahwah, NJ: Erlbaum.

Raudenbush, S. W. (2005). Learning from attempts to improve schooling: The contribution of methodological diversity. *Educational Researcher, 34*(5), 25–31.

Risley, T. R., & Wolf, M. M. (1973). Strategies for analyzing behavior change over time. In J. R. Nesselroade & H. W. Reese (Eds.), *Life-span developmental psychology: Methodological issues* (pp. 175–183). New York, NY: Academic Press.

Robinson, V. M. J. (1993). *Problem-based methodology: Research for the improvement of practice.* Oxford: Pergamon Press.

Robinson, V. M. J., & Lai, M. K. (2006). *Practitioner research for educators: A guide to improving classrooms and schools.* Thousand Oaks, CA: Corwin Press.

Robinson, V. M. J., Lloyd, C., & Rowe, K. J. (2008). The impact of leadership on student outcomes: An analysis of the differential effects of leadership type. *Educational Administration Quarterly, 44*(5), 635–674.

Rogoff, B. (2003). *The cultural nature of human development.* New York, NY: Oxford University Press.

Sanga, K., Reynolds, M., & Paulsen, I. (2018). Global comparative education. *Tok Stori, 2,* 3–19.

Scammacca, N., Roberts, G., Vaughn, S., Edmonds, M., Wexler, J., Reutebuch, C. K., & Torgesen, J. K. (2007). *Interventions for adolescent struggling readers: A meta-analysis with implications for practice.* Portsmouth: RMC Research Corporation, Center on Instruction.

Schildkamp, K., Handelzalts, A., Poortman, C. L., Leusink, H., Meerdink, M., Smit, M., … Hubers, M. D. (2018). *The Data Team™ procedure: A systematic approach to school improvement.* (Springer Texts in Education). Cham, Switzerland: Springer. https://doi.org/10.1007/978-3-319-58853-7

Schildkamp, K., & Kuiper, W. (2010). Data informed curriculum reform: Which data, what purposes, and promoting and hindering factors. *Teaching and Teacher Education, 26,* 482–496. doi:10.1016/j.tate.2009.06.007

Schildkamp, K., Poortman, C. L., & Handelzalts, A. (2016). Data teams for school improvement. *School effectiveness and school improvement, 27*(2), 228–254. doi:10.1080/09243453.2015.1056192

Schochet, P. Z., Puma, M., & Deke, J. (2014). *Understanding variation in treatment effects in education impact evaluations: An overview of quantitative methods. NCEE 2014–2017.* Washington, DC: National Center for Education Evaluation and Regional Assistance.

Schoenbach, R., Greenleaf, C., & Murphy, L. (2012). *Reading for understanding: How reading apprenticeship improves disciplinary learning in secondary and college classrooms* (2nd ed.). San Francisco, CA: Jossey-Bass.

Shadish, W. R., Cook, T. D., & Campbell, D. T. (2002). *Experimental and quasi-experimental designs for generalized causal inference.* Boston, MA: Houghton, Mifflin and Company.

Shanahan, T., & Shanahan, C. (2008). Teaching disciplinary literacy to adolescents: Rethinking content area literacy. *Harvard Education Review, 78,* 40–59.

Shulman, L. (1986). Those who understand: Knowledge growth in teaching. *Educational Researcher, 15*(2), 4–14. doi:10.3102/0013189X015002004

Sidman, M. (1960). *Tactics of scientific research: Evaluating experimental data in psychology* (Vol. 5). New York, NY: Basic Books.

Slavin, R. E., Cheung, A., Groff, C., & Lake, C. (2008). Effective reading programs for middle and high schools: A best-evidence synthesis. *Reading Research Quarterly, 43*(3), 290–322. doi:10.1598/RRQ.43.3.4

Smith, L. T. (1999). *Decolonizing methodologies: Research and indigenous peoples.* New York, NY: St. Martins Press.

Snow, C. E. (2015). 2014 Wallace Foundation distinguished lecture: Rigor and realism: Doing educational science in the real world. *Educational Researcher, 44*(9), 460–466. doi:10.3102/0013189X15619166

Snow, C. E. (2016). The role of relevance in education research, as viewed by former presidents. *Educational Researcher*, *45*(2), 64–68. doi:10.3102/0013189X16638325

Solomon, J., & Tresman, S. (1999). A model for continued professional development: Knowledge, belief and action. *Journal of In-Service Education*, *25*(2), 307–319. doi:10.1080/13674589900200081

Sparks, D. (2004). Focusing staff development on improving the learning of all students. In G. Cawelti (Ed.), *Handbook of research on improving student achievement* (3rd ed., pp. 245–255). Alexandria, VA: Educational Research Service.

Taylor, B. M., Pearson, P. D., Peterson, D. S., & Rodriguez, M. C. (2005). The CIERA school change framework: An evidence-based approach to professional development and school reading improvement. *Reading Research Quarterly*, *40*(1), 40–69. doi:10.1598/RRQ.40.1.3

Tett, G. (2015). *The Silo effect: The peril of expertise and the promise of breaking down barriers*. New York, NY: Simon and Schuster.

Timperley, H. (2011). *Realizing the power of professional learning*. Maidenhead: McGraw-Hill Education (UK).

Timperley, H., Wilson, A., Barrar, H., & Fung, I. (2007). *Teacher professional learning and development: Best evidence synthesis iteration (BES)*. Wellington: Ministry of Education.

Toole, J. C., & Seashore-Louis, K. (2002). The role of professional learning communities in international education. In K. Leithwood & P. Hallinger (Eds.), *Second international handbook of educational leadership and administration* (pp. 245–279). Dordrecht: Kluwer Academic.

Treviño, E., Cortázar, A., & Godoy, F. (2018). Conclusiones y recomendaciones para la politica y la practica [Conclusions and recommendations for policy and practice]. In E.Treviño, E. Aguirre, & C. Varela (Eds.), *Un Buen Comienzo para los niños de Chile [A good start for the children of Chile]* (pp. 289–303). Santiago de Chile: Ediciones Universidad Diego Portales.

Vaioleti, T. M. (2006). Talanoa research methodology: A developing position on pacific research. *Waikato Journal of Education*, *12*, 21–34.

Valsiner, J. (2000). *Culture and human development*. London: Sage.

van den Akker, J., Gravemeijer, K., McKenney, S., & Nieveen, N. (2006). Introducing educational design research. In J. van den Akker, K. Gravemeijer, S. McKenney, & N. Nieveen (Eds.), *Educational design research* (pp. 3–7). New York, NY: Routledge.

Vescio, V., Ross, D., & Adams, A. (2007). A review of research on the impact of professional learning communities on teaching practice and student learning. *Teaching and Teacher Education*, *24*, 80–91. doi:10.1016/j.tate.2007.01.004

Wang, J., & Guthrie, J. T. (2004). Modeling the effects of intrinsic motivation, extrinsic motivation, amount of reading, and past reading achievement on text comprehension between U.S. and Chinese students. *Reading Research Quarterly*, *39*(2), 162–186. doi:10.1598/RRQ.39.2.2

Weiland, C., Sachs, J., McCormick, M., Hsueh, J., & Snow, C. (in press). "Fast response" research to address timely practice and policy questions. *The Future of Children*, *29*.

Wenger, E. (1998). *Communities of practice: Learning, meaning, and identity*. Cambridge: Cambridge University Press.

Whitty, G. (2008). *Teacher professionalism: What next?* London: Institute of Education, University of London.

Wilkinson, I. A. G. & Son, E. H. (2010). A dialogic turn in research on learning and teaching to comprehend. In M. L. Kamil, P. D. Pearson, E. Moje, & P. Afflerbach (Eds.), *Handbook of reading research* (Vol. 4, pp. 359–387). New York, NY: Routledge.

Williamson, R., & Jesson, R. (2017). Log on and blog: An exploratory study assessing the impact of holiday blogging on student literacy achievement. *English Teaching: Practice & Critique, 16* (2), 222–237. doi:10.1108/ETPC-03-2017-0036

Wilson, A., McNaughton, S., & Lai, M. K. (2011). Reading achievement over the transition to secondary school: Profiling a problem. In *Proceedings of the symposium on assessment and learner outcomes*, Wellington, New Zealand. Retrieved from https://www.victoria.ac.nz/education/pdf/jhc-symposium/Proceedings-of-the-Symposium-on-Assessment-and-Learner-Outcomes.pdf

Wilson, A., & Oldehaver, J. (2017). A pilot project to promote talk about text in senior secondary classrooms. *Literacy Forum NZ, 32*(2), 14–23. Retrieved from http://nzla.org.nz/issue/literacy-forum-nz/

Wood, D. (1998). *How children think and learn: The social contexts of cognitive development*. London: Blackwell Publishing.

Zimmerman, B.J. (2006). Development and adaptation of expertise: The role of self-regulatory processes and beliefs. In K.A. Ericsson, N. Charness, P.J. Feltovich, & R. R. Hoffman (Eds.), *The Cambridge Handbook of expertise and expert performance* (pp. 705–722). Cambridge: Cambridge University Press.

Index